DIY
Chalkboard
Crafts

FROM SILHOUETTE ART TO SPICE JARS,

MORE THAN *50*

CRAFTY *and* CREATIVE

chalkboard-paint ideas

· Lizette Schapekahm ·

Adamsmedia
Avon, Massachusetts

Published by
Adams Media, a division of F+W Media, Inc.
57 Littlefield Street, Avon, MA 02322. U.S.A.
www.adamsmedia.com

ISBN 10: 1-4405-6834-0
ISBN 13: 978-1-4405-6834-3
eISBN 10: 1-4405-6835-9
eISBN 13: 978-1-4405-6835-0

Printed in the United States of America.

10 9 8 7 6 5 4 3 2 1

Library of Congress Cataloging-in-Publication Data
Schapekahm, Lizette.
  DIY chalkboard crafts / Lizette Schapekahm.
     pages cm
  Includes index.
  ISBN-13: 978-1-4405-6834-3 (pbk.)
  ISBN-10: 1-4405-6834-0 (pbk.)
  ISBN-13: 978-1-4405-6835-0
  ISBN-10: 1-4405-6835-9
  1. Painting. 2. Handicraft. 3. Blackboards. I. Title.
  TT385.S29 2013
  745.7'23--dc23
                    2013030850

Readers are urged to take all appropriate precautions before undertaking any how-to task. Always read and follow instructions and safety warnings for all tools and materials, and call in a professional if the task stretches your abilities too far. Although every effort has been made to provide the best possible information in this book, neither the publisher nor the author is responsible for accidents, injuries, or damage incurred as a result of tasks undertaken by readers. This book is not a substitute for professional services.

Many of the designations used by manufacturers and sellers to distinguish their product are claimed as trademarks. Where those designations appear in this book and F+W Media was aware of a trademark claim, the designations have been printed with initial capital letters.

Photography by Lizette Schapekahm and Frank Rivera.
Spot art © 123rf.com.

This book is available at quantity discounts for bulk purchases.
For information, please call 1-800-289-0963.

Contents

Chapter Four: Celebratory Creations • 73

Chapter Five: Outdoor Undertakings • 95

Chapter Six: The Organized Chalkboard • 115

Chapter Seven: Holiday Fun • 139

Introduction

From weddings to birthday parties, playrooms to kitchens, chalkboards seem to be popping up anywhere and everywhere lately. As chalkboard paint has become widely available and inexpensive, its popularity has exploded and for good reason. It is easy to use and versatile. It can allow you to release your inner creative genius on almost any household object. If you're like me and you have a child or a couple of children, you'll find chalkboard paint provides an endless source of fun and entertainment for the kids.

This book is filled with chalkboard projects both big and small and will guide and hopefully inspire you to use chalkboard paint elsewhere around your home. Browse the tips and techniques chapter to find out how to achieve beautiful results when working with chalkboard paint. The tools of the trade section will list some of the essential tools you will need to get these projects done. Each project tutorial includes a detailed supply list and set of directions as well as additional decoration ideas, tips, and/or advice on how to take the project even further.

If you've never used chalkboard paint before, why not start with a quick and easy project, such as the paperweight, coasters, or napkin rings? These are sure to give you success and results you can be pleased with. Once you've mastered the basic techniques of using chalkboard paint, you can move on to bigger, more involved projects, such as the shadow box, table runner, or menu board. Or—and this is the really great part!—design a project of your own.

However you decide to use this book, I hope it sparks creativity in you so that you can make chalkboard projects for your home, your loved ones, and for yourself.

HOW TO USE THIS BOOK

In this book, you will find seven chapters dedicated to chalkboard paint. The first chapter, Paint Like a Pro! Tips and Techniques for Working with Chalkboard Paint, gives you some tips and "dos and do nots" for using chalkboard paint as well as an overview of some of the supplies you will need for most of the projects. The remaining chapters, Around the Home, Crafts with Children, Celebratory Creations, Outdoor Undertakings, The Organized Chalkboard, and Holiday Fun, give directions on how to create more than fifty big or small projects and incorporate the goodness that is chalkboard paint into them. Some of the projects are quick and easy and will require just a little bit of chalkboard paint. Others are a bit more involved and will require a little bit of elbow grease and some power tools, but will leave you with stunning results. Let's get started, shall we?

CHAPTER ONE

Paint Like a Pro!
Tips and Techniques for Working with Chalkboard Paint

Painting with chalkboard paint is easy; even children can do it (with proper supervision, of course). All you need are a few tips and techniques, the right tools of the trade, and a dollop of inspiration. Since chalkboard paint can be used on almost any smooth surface, the possibilities are almost endless! Be creative and use your imagination in these projects to transform those ordinary objects in your home. Also, use this book as a guide to creating your own chalkboard projects. Pick and choose what you like from this book, put your own spin on the projects, and most importantly, have fun!

GENERAL TIPS AND TECHNIQUES

Chalkboard paint can be used on almost any surface: wood, metal, glass, ceramic, clay, fabric, porcelain, plaster, cardboard, terra cotta, canvas, papier-mâché, and plastic. Always begin with a clean, dry surface. A vacuum and tack cloths remove almost all dust and debris from a surface. If you've never used chalkboard paint before, here are some general guidelines. Note that for best results, you should always follow the directions found on the label of your chalkboard paint. In addition, follow these guidelines:

- Smooth, flat surfaces provide the best places to apply chalkboard paint. Do not apply chalkboard paint to bumpy or rough surfaces.
- If painting on wood, make sure the surface is smooth before painting. Sand the surface beginning with a coarser-grit sandpaper, such as 120 grit, working your way up to 220-grit sandpaper if necessary.
- Priming plastics, metals, and bare wood before using chalkboard paint will decrease the likelihood of the paint chipping, flaking, or scratching off.
- If you're using primer, use the correct kind for your surface. (For example, use primer intended for metal for metal surfaces and plastic primer for plastic surfaces.)
- If using multisurface chalkboard paint on fabrics, always prewash the fabric with soap and water. Allow it to dry thoroughly before applying the paint. Testing a small section of the fabric before initial use is always a good idea. Chalkboard paint will not adhere to all fabrics, so read the instructions on the label before proceeding.
- Painter's tape will give you crisp, clean edges and help prevent any paint from leaking onto surfaces that you wish to remain paint free. Always remember to firmly press the tape down before painting. I find that FrogTape works best for any paint project.
- Should any paint accidently leak under your painter's tape, scrape it off the surface with a razor blade.
- All chalkboard paints are *not* created equal, especially when it comes to drying times. Be sure to read the manufacturer's instructions on the labels of your chalkboard paint to learn about waiting time in between coats of paint as well as how long it will take the paint to cure before you can season it. Some chalkboard paint will require the surface to cure for 24 hours before initial use.
- Always season a chalkboard surface before writing on it for the first time. To season a chalkboard, rub a piece of white chalk over the entire surface and then erase it. Do not use a chalk marker or colored chalk to season a chalkboard surface.
- If you want your writing to last a bit longer and not rub off so easily, use a chalk marker instead of a regular piece of chalk. To remove chalk marker from a chalkboard surface, use a damp paper towel or rag.
- When creating chalkboard-paint projects for children, make sure they don't contain anything harmful to babies or toddlers if they put

them in their mouths. Most chalkboard paint is nontoxic, but it is better to be safe than sorry!

Don't limit yourself to the basic black or green chalkboard colors. There are many colors of chalkboard paint available in craft and home improvement stores. You can also have chalkboard paint tinted to almost any color, making it useable in any color scheme in your home. So go wild!

There are many resources in books and on the Internet for making your own chalkboard paint. This isn't discussed in this book, but you might want to research and try it for yourself!

TIPS ON USING BRUSH-ON CHALKBOARD PAINT

There are two basic ways to apply chalkboard paint to a surface: brushing and spraying. Here are some tips about brush-on paint:

- Follow all instructions found on the label before beginning any paint project.
- Before using brush-on chalkboard paint, stir the paint well with a paint stick. To prevent any bubbles, avoid shaking the paint or stirring too vigorously.
- Foam paintbrushes (or foam rollers for large surfaces) work well for most projects, allowing for easy application and providing a smooth-finished product.
- When using brush-on chalkboard paint, two or three thin coats are better than one or two thick ones.

- When applying chalkboard paint with a paintbrush, keep a wet edge to prevent lap marks and raised edges, which might show once you have seasoned your chalkboard surface and start writing on it.

TIPS ON USING CHALKBOARD SPRAY PAINT

Follow all instructions found on the label before beginning any paint project. In addition:

- Protect any and all surfaces from overspray and always spray in a well-ventilated area. Don't forget those masks and safety glasses to protect your nose, mouth, and eyes!
- Shake the can well for 1–2 minutes before each application.
- When using chalkboard spray paint, two or three thin coats are better than one or two thick ones.
- When using chalkboard spray paint, for best results use smooth strokes and keep the paint can 8–10" away from the surface you are spraying.
- Chalkboard spray paint is not yet low VOC (which stands for Volatile Organic Compound)—that is, it emits gases that can injure your health if breathed in large enough quantities. To prevent any toxic fumes from entering your home, leave the piece you have painted outside or in the garage for 24 hours. This is especially important when creating chalkboard projects for children.

TIPS ON USING PORCELAIN CHALKBOARD PAINT

There's a special version of chalkboard paint made especially for use on porcelain; we'll work with it in some of the projects in this book. Here are some suggestions for its use:

- Follow all instructions found on the label before beginning any paint project.
- Porcelain chalkboard paint requires an oven to cure the paint, which will enable you to put the finished project in the microwave and dishwasher. The majority of porcelain paint brands require you to bake most small projects for 30 minutes at 32°F. Be sure to read and follow the directions provided by the manufacturer.
- Porcelain chalkboard paint is best applied with a natural-bristle paintbrush.

TOOLS OF THE TRADE

The majority of the supplies and tools you will need to use in this book are standard and easy to use. You don't need any special skills to use chalkboard paint—just a little time, patience, and creativity! Here is a list of a few of the basic tools and craft supplies you will need. More detailed lists can be found at the beginning of each project.

- Chalkboard paint, in the form of brush-on paint, spray paint, or porcelain paint

- Spray paint primer as well as various colors of spray paint
- Something to protect your work surface, such as a drop cloth, newspaper, or cardboard
- Wood found at craft and home improvement stores
- Foam paintbrushes or rollers in various sizes
- A pair of scissors, a ruler, a hammer, a saw, a drill, clamps, wire cutters, a razor blade, and needle-nose pliers
- Sandpaper of varying grits and tack cloths
- Glue (both wood glue and hot glue)
- Washi tape, twine, thin-gauge wire, baker's twine, and glitter
- Oven-bake clay, a crafting rolling pin, and cookie cutters
- Chalk and chalk markers and an eraser
- Battery-operated LED tea lights

TIPS FOR BUILDING PROJECTS

A few words about the projects before we get started:

- If you don't have some of the tools listed for a project, don't worry. Most of the projects can be created with smaller power tools or hand tools. This is a great opportunity to get your hands dirty.
- For the projects requiring wood, I used pine most frequently because it is inexpensive and easy to find in various lengths, widths, and thicknesses. Feel free to substitute the wood of your choice.

- A combination square is a very useful tool to have on hand for the building projects in this book, helping you keep everything straight and square. It is also the perfect tool to use for lay-out marks, keeping your work more uniform.
- A larger 12" compound miter saw/sliding compound miter saw and circular saw/trim saw can replace a table saw in most of these projects.
- Scour local building supply or craft stores to find boards that are already the size you want or close to it. You may have to change the dimensions of the project slightly to accommodate your materials, however, but that's part of the fun, isn't it? Make the projects your own.
- None of the projects in this book need to support a lot of weight (with the exception of the stool), so wood glue alone, held in place with clamps until it dries, will work for most of the projects. However, reinforcing the glued joints with brad nails or pin nails gives each piece some additional strength. Use your discretion, and remember: safety first.
- A jigsaw fitted with a scroll saw blade can replace a scroll saw.
- The notches for the art caddy and seed box can be cut using a fine-tooth handsaw.
- Always wipe off excess glue before it dries.
- Square butt joints are used for the building projects in this book. Although these joints are not the strongest woodworking joints to use, they are simple to make and will work just fine on these smaller projects.
- Make sure to read and follow the manufacturer's directions that come with any power and hand tools. Safety glasses are a must for the building projects and wearing a dust mask will certainly keep your lungs happy. Always work safely.

ADDITIONAL INSPIRATION

Here are some additional ideas for chalkboard projects not included in this book. They may help you to find other surfaces around the home you can paint with chalkboard paint:

- Piggy bank
- Toy box
- Gallery wall
- Kitchen backsplash
- Cupboards
- Wall border
- Headboard
- Staircase treads
- Desk
- Placemats
- Magnets
- Thermos
- Picture frames
- Gift boxes

Whatever crafts and projects from this book you decide to create and make over for your home or for others, I hope you enjoy the process of chalkboard-paint crafting. There is something very special and rewarding about using an object you made with your own hands, especially when you share it with those who mean the most to you.

CHAPTER TWO

Around the Home

Look around you. How many places in your home can you find that would be enhanced with a chalkboard? Now go through the projects in this chapter. You can put the coasters, globe, and coffee-table spheres on your coffee table, bookshelves, or mantel. The mug and menu board will fit seamlessly into your kitchen. The vase filler and succulent terrarium will spruce up any dining or end table in any room. Don't have a place to put your books and magazines? No worries! Make yourself a chalkboard bookcase. These projects will make any room in your home a fun and enjoyable space.

WALL SCONCE
and LAMP SHADE

Every house needs a cozy reading corner with a wall sconce and a chalkboard-painted lamp shade—somewhere you can cuddle up with a book on a rainy afternoon. The painted glass shade of a wall sconce will give off a soft glow, providing the perfect amount of light for reading. There are many new and used wall sconces available in a wide price range. This project gives you a unique way to combine function and style while brightening up a dark corner of a room.

What You'll Need:

- ○ Wall sconce
- ○ Glass shade (style and shape is up to you; just make sure it fits in the wall sconce)
- ○ 1" painter's tape
- ○ Chalkboard paint
- ○ 1" foam paintbrush
- ○ Chalk

What You'll Do:

1. Install the wall sconce on a wall, following the manufacturer's directions provided with the sconce. If necessary, hire an electrician to do this step for you.

2. Next, decide how much of the glass shade you would like to paint with the chalkboard paint. Tape off the portion you don't want painted, using the painter's tape. I chose to paint the bottom third of my glass shade so the sconce would give off enough light to see and read by.

3. Using the foam paintbrush, apply 2–3 coats of chalkboard paint to the outside of the glass lamp shade. Be sure to read the manufacturer's instructions on the label for drying times in between each coat of paint.

4. Season the chalkboard by rubbing a piece of chalk over the entire surface and then erasing it. You are now ready to write on your lamp shade.

Placing the wall sconce in a guest bedroom provides a simple and beautiful way to leave a welcoming message or reminder for your guests. Using a chalkboard-painted lamp shade in a child's bedroom is a helpful way to remind them that it's "lights out at eight" or to "make the bed."

SILHOUETTE ART

A silhouette is a classic art form; you may be surprised at how easy it is to make. When you add a chalkboard element to these silhouettes, it keeps the dark traditional look of a silhouette but uses black chalkboard paint instead of black paper. Place these silhouettes in an entryway, kitchen, or mudroom and you've got a dedicated place in which to leave messages and reminders for family members. Not only that, but since these silhouettes are made from sturdy plywood, they will stand up to use. Beautiful and functional: What more could you ask from a piece of art?

What You'll Need:

- ○ Scissors or craft knife
- ○ A photograph of you or a loved one, taken in profile and printed out onto a piece of paper or card stock
- ○ Masking tape
- ○ ¼"-thick plywood with at least one smooth side, measuring at least 11" × 8½"
- ○ Pencil
- ○ Scroll saw (or coping saw)
- ○ Dremel (optional) (or other rotary tool with 120-grit round sanding attachment)
- ○ Metal file (optional)
- ○ Sandpaper (120, 150, 220 grit)
- ○ Chalkboard paint
- ○ Foam paintbrush (1" or smaller, depending on the size of your photograph)
- ○ Chalk
- ○ Picture-hanging hardware, such as a steel sawtooth ring hanger (optional) (rated for 20 pounds)

What You'll Do:

1. Using the scissors or craft knife, carefully cut out the picture you've printed onto heavy paper or cardstock as you would like it to appear in the finished silhouette. Work carefully while completing this step because even a small detail such as an eyelash or a curl can make a big difference in the final look of the silhouette.

2. Tape your cut-out paper silhouette to the smooth, finished side of the plywood. Carefully trace around the image in pencil, again paying attention to those details.

3. Once the image is traced, remove the paper from the plywood. Check to make sure the outline of the image looks just the way you want it to. It will be much easier to make changes with a pencil now rather than after you have cut it.

4. Using your saw, carefully cut around the image, leaving your pencil line visible (you will sand down to this line later). A scroll saw is the perfect choice for a project like this because the blade is thin and flexible so you can easily maneuver into those small details. If you do not have access to a scroll saw, a coping saw will also work well. Take your time cutting out the image; avoid chip-out from the saw. What you'll wind up with is your piece of 8½" × 11" plywood with a silhouette cut out from it.

5. Once the main cuts are made, you are ready for sanding. If you have a rotary tool such as a Dremel, fitted with a #438 ¼" 120-grit sanding band attachment, this will make this step easier. Turn the Dremel to a low speed and carefully run it along the edge of the silhouette right down to your pencil line. This will produce a nice, smooth, finished edge. If you don't have a Dremel, you can do the sanding by hand, using 120-grit sandpaper. For those really narrow areas, small metal files and sandpaper will help you get the job done. Sand until you are satisfied with the results.

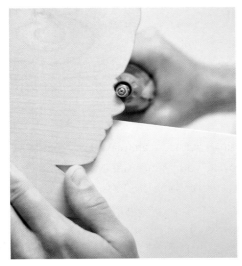

7. Once the paint has dried, season the silhouette by taking a small piece of chalk and rubbing it over the entire portion of the chalkboard silhouette and then erasing it. You are now ready to write on your chalkboard silhouette art.

8. If you want to hang your silhouette on a wall, install the picture-hanging hardware on the back of your silhouette. Otherwise, enjoy the silhouette on a shelf, table, or bookcase.

Be creative with this project! Use photographs that hold special meaning to you. Print off a silhouette photo of each of your children or a family pet. Draw in baby curls, ribbons or bow ties with the chalk. Hang the silhouettes near an entry door and use them as a space to leave messages for members of the family. Find old photographs of grandparents and great-grandparents and create a family tree gallery wall with the full names of each family member beneath his or her silhouette. The creative possibilities are endless!

6. Now that the wood has been cut and sanded, you are ready to paint. With the foam paintbrush, apply 2–3 coats of chalkboard paint to the silhouette. Be sure to read the manufacturer's instructions on the label for drying times between each coat of paint.

GLOBE

A globe is a timeless decorative (and educational) addition to any room. You can spend hours staring at one, imagining all the places you could go or have been. It can also easily make a room trendy, classy, beautiful, or just plain cute. This project will allow you to take those characteristics even further as you create a useful and beautiful decoration. If you have children, use the chalkboard globe to test their knowledge of geography or history. However you decide to use your chalkboard globe, you can be sure that it will be a welcome feature of any space in your home!

What You'll Need:

- Globe
- Chalkboard paint
- ½"–1" foam paintbrush
- White paint marker
- Chalk

What You'll Do:

1. Decide how much of your globe you are going to cover with chalkboard paint. I chose to leave the outline of each continent in order to make drawing in the continents much easier later on by simply painting around them with the chalkboard paint. You can also trace over the original outline of the continents with a paint pen.

2. Paint over the desired portions of the globe with 2–3 coats of chalkboard paint until there are no visible paint streaks. Be sure to read the manufac-turer's instructions on the label for drying times in between each coat of paint.

3. Once the paint has dried, use the paint pen to draw the outline of each continent that you left while painting. If you do not want the outlines of each continent to be permanent, use a chalk marker instead.

4. Season the chalkboard-painted portions of the globe by rubbing them with a piece of chalk and then erasing it. You are now ready to write on your chalkboard globe.

Don't limit yourself to globes! Find an old class-room map of the United States, paint it with chalk-board paint, and record family vacations on it. Map out the road trip you took on your honeymoon. Or, go smaller by finding a map of your state and record-ing your family camping trips. Think of something that has meaning to you.

BOOKCASE

Do you have difficulty keeping the books on your bookshelves organized? If so, this project is perfect for you. After painting the back of any bookcase with chalkboard paint, you can label its sections to keep it more orderly. The added benefit of the black-painted back portion of this bookcase is that it makes the books and other décor on the shelves really stand out, giving you a beautiful as well as functional result.

What You'll Need:

- ○ Bookcase
- ○ 1"–2" wide painter's tape
- ○ Primer (optional)
- ○ Chalkboard paint
- ○ Paintbrush or roller (size dependent on how large a surface area you need to paint)
- ○ Chalk

What You'll Do:

1. Prep your bookcase for painting. With the painter's tape, tape off any portions of the bookcase that you wish to remain unpainted. If necessary, prime the back of the bookcase.

2. Paint 2–3 coats of chalkboard paint onto the back portion of the bookcase. Be sure to read the manufacturer's instructions on the label for drying times in between each coat of paint.

3. After the chalkboard paint has dried, you are ready to season the bookcase. Take a piece of chalk, rub the entire chalkboard surface, and then erase it. You are now ready to write on your chalkboard bookcase.

Don't limit yourself to organizing your books by alphabetical order! Why not organize by categories, giving such labels as biographies, fiction, history, etc.? Once you've organized them into categories, then put them into alphabetical order within each category, either by author or by title. This can be especially helpful on a child's bookcase in her bedroom. It will not only help the child find what she is looking for but it will enable her to put away her books more easily. What's not to love about that?

LIGHT-UP HOUSES

There's something magical about the silhouette of a big city skyline, especially at night when all of the lights twinkle against the dark outlines of the buildings. Now you can bring some of that magic into your home by creating your own skyline. And the best part is you can make it look any way you want—it comes from your imagination.

Note: Poplar was used in this project, but any other kind of wood will do. I don't recommend that you use plywood for this project because of the rough edges.

What You'll Need:

WOOD FOR SQUARE HOUSE:
- Top (1): 3½" × 3½" × ¼"
- Front and back (2): 3½" × 3½" × ¼"
- Sides (2): 3½" × 3" × ¼"

WOOD FOR RECTANGLE HOUSE:
- Top (1): 5½" × 3" × ¼"
- Front and back (2): 5½" × 3" × ¼"
- Sides (2): 3½" × 3" × ¼"

WOOD FOR SLANTED-ROOF HOUSE:
- Roof (1): 3⅜" × 2½" × ¼" (both edges mitered to fit 45° roof pitch)
- Front and Back (2): 7½" × 2½" × ¼"
- Long/Left Side (1): 7¼" × 2½" × ¼" (one edge mitered to fit the 45° roof pitch)
- Short/Right Side (1): 5" × 2½" × ¼"

OTHER SUPPLIES
- Tape measure
- Pencil
- Table saw (or compound miter saw if your wood does not need to be ripped)
- Drill
- ¼" drill bit
- Scroll saw
- Small metal file (optional)
- Sandpaper (150, 220 grit)
- Wood glue
- Clamps (3 or more)
- Chalkboard spray paint
- Chalk
- Chalk marker
- 3 battery-operated LED tea lights

SQUARE HOUSE

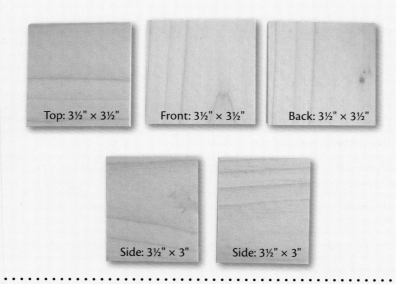

Top: 3½" × 3½"

Front: 3½" × 3½"

Back: 3½" × 3½"

Side: 3½" × 3"

Side: 3½" × 3"

RECTANGLE HOUSE

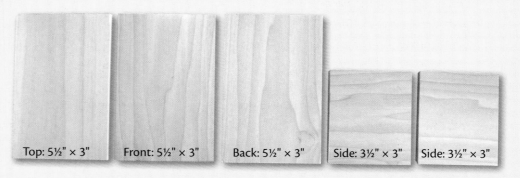

Top: 5½" × 3"

Front: 5½" × 3"

Back: 5½" × 3"

Side: 3½" × 3"

Side: 3½" × 3"

SLANTED-ROOF HOUSE

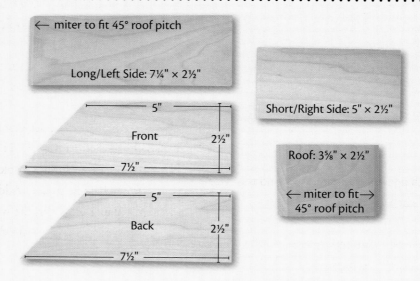

← miter to fit 45° roof pitch

Long/Left Side: 7¼" × 2½"

Short/Right Side: 5" × 2½"

5"

Front

2½"

7½"

Roof: 3⅝" × 2½"

← miter to fit →
45° roof pitch

5"

Back

2½"

7½"

What You'll Do:

1. Cut out the pieces for each house according to the dimensions listed in the materials list. You may want to make a sketch first to guide you. Pay special attention to the measurements for the slanted-roof house, since they are a bit tricky. On each piece, draw windows and doors. Label each piece to make assembly easier.

2. When the pieces are cut out and you have drawn on your windows and doors, drill a hole near the corner of one of the window or door openings with the ¼" drill bit. Then, insert the scroll saw blade through the hole and cut out the remainder of the door or window. Repeat for additional doors and windows. An alternative method, if you don't have a scroll saw, is to drill a series of holes in a row within the door or window. Then, using a metal file, remove the remainder of the material.

3. After each piece is cut out, lightly sand the edges to remove any rough spots.

4. Using the wood glue and clamps, put the houses together. Take care to wipe up any excess glue that may have gathered at the seams to keep things neat and tidy.

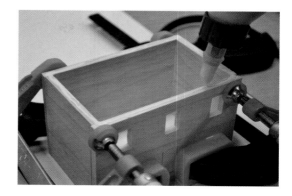

5. After you have given the wood glue sufficient time to dry (read the label for drying times), spray paint the inside and outside of each house with 2–3 coats of the chalkboard spray paint.

6. When the spray paint has dried, season each house by rubbing them with a piece of chalk and then erasing them.

7. Using a chalk marker, decorate each house with fun accents, such as bricks, shingles, windows, etc.

8. Set a battery-operated tea light inside each house and watch them glow!

These are fun for any season, but they're especially festive during the Halloween and Christmas holidays. Draw little pumpkins or Christmas wreaths onto each little house. Adding special touches like tissue-paper ghosts in the windows or artificial snow on the rooftops will make them adorable.

COASTERS

Cocktail parties are great fun, but not so much if guests leave glass rings on your good furniture. Chalkboard coasters can help not only to keep your coffee table ring free, but also they can make it easier for your guests to keep track of their drinks. Place some brand-new pieces of chalk in a small decorative bowl next to the coasters so that your guests can personalize their coaster themselves. Get their creative juices flowing by offering a prize for the most creative coaster. It's a party, after all!

What You'll Need:

- ○ Wooden coasters
- ○ Painter's tape (width dependent on the size of your coaster)
- ○ Chalkboard paint
- ○ 1" foam paintbrush
- ○ Chalk

What You'll Do:

1. Tape off any portions of your coasters that you wish to remain free of paint.

2. Paint 2–3 thin coats of chalkboard paint onto each coaster. Be sure to read the manufacturer's instructions on the label for drying times in between each coat of paint.

3. Once the paint has dried, season each coaster with a piece of chalk by rubbing and then erasing it. You are now ready to write on your chalkboard coasters.

For even more do-it-yourself fun, purchase some inexpensive square wooden tiles and paint them with chalkboard paint. Cut squares, rectangles, circles, or any shape you like out of the wood and make your own coasters from scratch to create a unique look. Don't forget to protect your furniture by placing some felt pads on the bottom of the coasters to prevent scratching.

COFFEE-TABLE
SPHERES

Some people say that a perfectly styled coffee table has three or more of the following items: fresh flowers, hardcover books, a fragrant candle, and something to "catch the eye." This project catches the eye all right—it allows you to get creative with your coffee-table décor. Place these chalkboard coffee-table spheres in a beautiful bowl on your coffee table after you've decorated them to your heart's desire. You're on your way to a perfectly styled coffee table.

What You'll Need:

- ○ Smooth white Styrofoam spheres (size and quantity up to you)
- ○ A razor blade
- ○ Chalkboard spray paint
- ○ Chalk
- ○ Chalk marker

What You'll Do:

1. With the razor blade carefully remove the raised seam around the circumference of each Styrofoam sphere.

2. In a well-ventilated area, apply 2–3 coats of chalkboard spray paint to each sphere. Be sure to read the manufacturer's instructions on the label for drying times in between each coat of paint.

3. When the paint has dried completely, season each sphere by rubbing it with a piece of chalk and then erasing it.

You are now ready to decorate your coffee-table spheres. Place them in your favorite bowl with a small bowl of chalk next to them. Then you'll be able to decorate whenever your creative heart desires.

Get creative with your doodles! Draw some fun checkerboard, chevron, or polka-dot patterns on each sphere. Jot down a few of your favorite quotes. Set them out during a party and allow your guests to decorate them or leave messages of their own.

VASE FILLER

Some plants, such as calla lilies and tulips, have stems that are almost as beautiful as their flowers. However, there are others where the stems are less appealing and can give your bouquet a messy look. To hide those unattractive stems, as well as give your next bouquet more visual pizzazz, make this easy chalkboard vase filler. What I especially like about it is that you can personalize it, making it suitable for any season or occasion.

What You'll Need:

- ○ Clear glass cylinder-style vase (size and quantity up to you)
- ○ Thin, pliable tag board or cardboard (a large cereal box works well)
- ○ Ruler
- ○ Scissors
- ○ 1" foam paintbrush
- ○ Chalkboard paint
- ○ Small jar(s) (should be able to fit inside the vase(s) above)
- ○ Chalk
- ○ Flowers

What You'll Do:

1. Measure and cut the cardboard so that it will fit inside of your vase.

2. Next, use the foam paintbrush to paint 2–3 coats of chalkboard paint onto the cardboard. Be sure to read the manufacturer's instructions on the label for drying times in between each coat of paint.

3. When the paint has dried, season the chalkboard by rubbing it with a piece of chalk and erasing it.

4. Now get creative with your chalkboard filler. Why not draw different designs or write a favorite quote on it? Or write the various types of flowers contained in your bouquet. Your creativity and imagination are your only limit.

5. Next, fill the small jar with water and carefully place it inside the vase. If you are worried about spilling, set the jar in the vase first and then fill it with water. Check to make sure your main vase is dry.

6. Carefully slide your decorated chalkboard design inside the vase.

7. Arrange your flowers inside the jar and enjoy.

A small grouping of these on your dining room table will be especially beautiful.

Menu Board

:∴ MENU ∴:

Monday: White Chicken Chili,
Tortilla Chips, &
Guacamole

Tuesday: Bleu Cheese Burgers,
Oven Fries, & Salad

Wednesday: Spaghetti and
Meatballs & Green Beans

Thursday: Cajun Chicken Wraps
& Potato Chips

Friday: Salmon, Wild Rice,
& Roasted Asparagus

Saturday: Pizza night!

Sunday: Pot Roast, Garli
Mashed Potatoes, Br

Almost every woman knows that food is first and foremost in a man's mind. I live with three boys: my husband and our two small sons. I hear the question, "What's for dinner?" too many times during the day to keep track of. To keep myself sane, I use this simple menu board in my kitchen. This handy kitchen tool can help make meal planning much easier. The whole family will love this!

What You'll Need:

- ○ 12" × 18" × ½" plywood with at least one finished/sanded side. (Any type of wood can be used for this, but plywood is an inexpensive option with a large surface to paint and write on.)
- ○ Wood filler
- ○ Sandpaper (150, 220 grit)
- ○ Tack cloth
- ○ Compound miter saw or miter box with saw
- ○ 1" lattice trim measuring approximately 65" in length
- ○ Pencil
- ○ Chalkboard paint
- ○ Gray semigloss paint
- ○ 1" and 2" foam paintbrushes
- ○ Wood glue
- ○ Clamps
- ○ Brad nailer (or pin nailer)
- ○ ½" brad nails or ½" pin nails)
- ○ Chalk

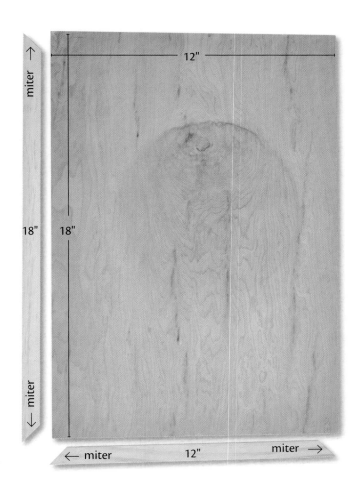

What You'll Do:

1. Because plywood often has rough edges with gaps in the wood, fill in the sides of the plywood using wood filler. Let dry for at least 15 minutes.

2. Sand the edges smooth using 150-grit sandpaper and finishing with 220 grit. Clean up any dust and debris with the tack cloth.

3. Miter cut your 1" lattice trim pieces to fit along the edges of the plywood. The long/outside edge of the miter cut is 18" on the two vertical pieces and 12" on the two horizontal pieces. Although miter cuts were used here, if you are uncomfortable making these cuts, you could always use square butt joints, which are straight square cuts, for the trim instead. Dry fit your pieces to the plywood, checking to make sure everything fits tightly. Label the back side of these mitered frame pieces so you can easily reassemble them later.

4. Apply 2–3 coats of chalkboard paint to the sanded side of the plywood and to the edges. Be sure to read the manufacturer's instructions on the label for drying times in between each coat of paint. Applying chalkboard paint now will eliminate the need to tape off areas for painting later.

5. To make finishing easier, paint your trim pieces with 2–3 coats of the gray semigloss paint before installing them. Once you are satisfied with the coverage and the paint is dry, glue and clamp your trim pieces in place. The glue will do the work of holding everything together, but if you would like, use ½" brad nails or ½" pin nails to help hold the trim in place.

6. Once the glue has dried, remove the clamps. Fill in any nail holes or other imperfections with wood filler and sand smooth. Clean up any dust and debris with the tack cloth.

7. Touch up any portions of the frame with additional paint, if necessary.

8. To season the chalkboard surface, rub a piece of chalk over the entire surface and then erase it.

You are now ready to use your chalkboard paint–covered menu board. Hang it in your kitchen in a prominent space where everyone can see it, enjoy it, and always know what's for dinner.

COFFEE MUG

Your morning java will taste *soooo* much better when it's in a chalkboard-decorated mug, with something written on it about coffee making the world go round. It's not only useful for everyday use in your home, but these mugs will make excellent stocking stuffers, gifts for the bride and groom, or even your child's teacher.

What You'll Need:

- ○ A plain coffee mug
- ○ 1" painter's tape
- ○ Porcelain chalkboard paint
- ○ Small, natural-bristle paintbrush
- ○ Oven
- ○ Baking sheet
- ○ Parchment paper
- ○ Oven mitts
- ○ Chalk

What You'll Do:

Note: **Before beginning this project, please follow the instructions found on the bottle of your porcelain chalkboard paint.**

1. Wash and dry the mug thoroughly.

2. Tape off any portions of the mug that you wish to remain free of paint. Take care to press the tape down firmly to prevent the paint from leaking underneath.

3. Apply 2–3 thin coats of the porcelain chalkboard paint with the paintbrush, allowing for sufficient drying time between each coat of paint. Follow the directions on the label of your porcelain paint bottle for drying times.

4. Remove the painter's tape and allow at least 24 hours of drying time after the last coat of paint before baking it in the oven.

5. Place the coffee mug on a parchment paper–covered baking sheet before putting it into a preheated oven. Most porcelain chalkboard paint requires you to bake the mug at 300°F for 30 minutes and allow the mug to cure at room temperature for 24 hours before washing and using. Again, for best results I recommend following the directions on the label of your porcelain chalkboard-paint bottle. Baking the coffee mug will allow you to use it in the microwave as well as wash it in the dishwasher.

6. Before drawing on the coffee mug, season the chalkboard portion of the mug by rubbing it with a piece of chalk and then erasing it.

Use this porcelain chalkboard paint on any dish in your kitchen, such as a plate, platter, or bowl.

Succulent Terrarium

Sempervivum

Things that are growing enhance any room. And a terrarium is a wonderful, low-maintenance way to bring something green into your living room. While you're at it, why not liven it up with some chalkboard paint?

What You'll Need:

- Glass vase or bowl (any shape of your choice)
- 1"–2" painter's tape
- Chalkboard paint
- 1" foam paintbrush
- Chalk
- Small stones or pebbles
- Activated charcoal
- Potting soil
- Succulents (as many as your container will allow)
- Spray bottle filled with water

What You'll Do:

1. Wash the glass vase and dry thoroughly.

2. Tape off the top two-thirds of the vase with painter's tape, taking care to press the edge of the tape down firmly so that no paint will leak under it while painting.

3. Using your chalkboard paint, paint the bottom third of the vase. Give it as many coats of chalkboard paint as necessary until you are no longer able to see any streaks and are unable to see through the chalkboard paint. Let the chalk-board paint dry thoroughly in between each coat. Read the label on your chalkboard paint for drying times.

4. After the chalkboard paint has dried, season the vase by rubbing the painted area with a piece of chalk and then erasing it.

5. To make your terrarium garden, first place a 1" layer of stones in the bottom of the vase.

6. Next, place a 1" layer of the activated charcoal on top of the stones.

7. Then, place a 3"–4" layer of the potting soil on top of the charcoal. This layer should be a bit thicker than the previous two, since this is where you will plant the succulents.

8. Using your fingers, make a small hole in the potting soil and place a succulent in the hole. Repeat this step until you have planted all of your succulents.

9. After your succulents are planted, use the spray bottle to gently water them.

Now you are ready to use the chalkboard portion of the terrarium. You can write the name of each succulent in your terrarium. Or, you can write a famous quote or saying about gardening, such as the Chinese proverb, "He who plants a garden, plants happiness." Do you want the chalkboard portion to serve a more decorative purpose? If so, draw a fun chevron border or some polka dots on the container. If you want the chalkboard portion to serve a more functional purpose, you can write the date of each watering in order to better care for your plants. If succulents aren't your thing, feel free to substitute your favorite plants instead!

CHAPTER THREE

Crafts with Children

Small hands are great at playing make-believe and creating messes. The projects in this chapter all have a child in mind. You can work on some of these projects with children or surprise them with a gift they will always treasure. In any case, you'll find that children are an endless source of creativity. It seems a shame that when we grow up, most of us lose a lot of this childlike spontaneity, but I hope that with these projects, you'll rediscover your inner child.

PLAY TABLE

You know . . . you *know* . . . that sooner or later your children are going to write on something they shouldn't—a wall, table, couch. It's inevitable. Every child does it. Why not enable that spontaneous creativity by giving them the perfect piece of furniture on which they can draw and write and *not* get into trouble? By painting a child-size play table, you can provide hours of fun and entertainment for your children while at the same time saving your furniture and sanity!

What You'll Need:

- ○ 1"–2" painter's tape
- ○ Child-size table
- ○ Spray paint primer
- ○ Chalkboard spray paint
- ○ Chalk

What You'll Do:

1. Using the painter's tape, tape off any portions of the table that you don't want covered with the primer or chalkboard paint, such as the sides or legs.

2. In a well-ventilated area, spray the top of the table with 2 coats of primer, allowing for sufficient drying time between each coat. Read the label on your primer for appropriate drying times. Using the primer will make the chalkboard-painted surface more durable and resistant to those inevitable bangs and bumps from toys.

3. After the primer has dried, paint 2–3 coats of chalkboard paint onto the tabletop.

4. When the paint has dried, season the tabletop by rubbing it with a piece of chalk and then erasing it.

Go ahead. Tell your kids to write on the furniture!

PUZZLE

I See the Moon and the Moon Sees Me

God bless the moon and God bless me!

Puzzles are great for long, rainy afternoons when it's too wet to play outside. And kids will jump at the chance to create their own jigsaw puzzle. Creating a chalkboard puzzle will allow children endless opportunities for creativity. Find a blank wooden or cardboard puzzle and give it a facelift with some chalkboard paint. Wrap the puzzle up with a brand-new box of multicolored chalk and a cute little eraser, perfect for tiny hands. You just made gift giving a little easier on yourself and a lot of fun for the one who will receive it!

What You'll Need:

- ○ Wooden or cardboard puzzle
- ○ Chalkboard spray paint
- ○ Chalk

What You'll Do:

1. Take the puzzle apart. Separate and spread the pieces out on a well-protected work surface, making sure the pieces are not touching. Before painting, check that all of the pieces are "picture" side up.

2. In a well-ventilated area, spray 1–2 thin coats of chalkboard paint. Read the manufacturer's instructions on the label to find out how long you will need to allow the paint to dry in between coats.

3. When the paint has dried overnight, put the puzzle back together.

4. Season the puzzle by rubbing it with a piece of chalk and erasing it. You are now ready to draw your own picture on the puzzle.

Encourage kids to erase your picture after they've put the puzzle together and draw their own.

BUILDING BLOCKS

Children of all ages love to play with blocks, but buying a quality set of these toys can be expensive. However, it's easy, fun, and inexpensive to make your own. By incorporating chalkboard paint into this project, you make these blocks customizable and a lot more fun for the little ones in your life. The addition of polyurethane on a portion of each block gives them a decorative and modern look. Since you made them yourself, they'll become a much-loved toy that will surely be passed on to future generations.

What You'll Need:

- ○ Tape measure
- ○ Pencil
- ○ Poplar measuring 2" square × 36" long. This is how this piece is sold at the home store. From this 36"-long piece of poplar, you will cut cubes that are 2" × 2" × 2".
- ○ Compound miter saw or table saw
- ○ Sandpaper (150, 220 grit)
- ○ Tack cloth
- ○ Clear-gloss fast-drying polyurethane
- ○ 2 1" foam paintbrushes
- ○ Painter's tape (optional)
- ○ Chalkboard paint
- ○ Chalk
- ○ Chalk marker

What You'll Do:

1. Using the compound miter saw or table saw, cut the poplar square into cubes measuring 2" × 2" × 2" with the saw. For this project, I made 10 blocks. However, the poplar square will allow for approximately 17 blocks.

2. Using the sandpaper, sand away any rough edges and make sure that all sides of the block are smooth to the touch. Begin sanding with the 150 grit and end with the 220 grit for the smoothest finish. Wipe away any dust and debris with the tack cloth.

3. Decide on which two sides of each block you are going to apply the polyurethane, taking care to choose the sides with the most attractive wood grain, since these are the ones that will be seen. The two sides should be opposite each other. Apply the polyurethane with a foam paintbrush. For best results, follow the manufacturer's instructions, which will help you determine how many coats to use as well as how long it will take for the polyurethane to dry.

4. After the polyurethane has dried, paint the remainder of the sides of each block with the chalkboard paint, taking care to allow for drying time in between each coat of paint. Use painter's tape if you are worried about getting chalkboard paint on the sides that have polyurethane on them. Each block will require 2–3 coats of paint.

5. Season each chalkboard side of the blocks by rubbing it with a piece of chalk and then erasing it. You are now ready to write on your chalkboard blocks.

Make a couple of sets of these at a time to prepare yourself for those inevitable baby shower and birthday party gifts. You can also get creative by using various colors of chalkboard paint, which will be especially appealing to small children.

HOUSE-SHAPED COAT HOOK

Inspire your kids to clean up after themselves by making an adorable chalkboard coat hook. What a fun addition this will be to a child's bedroom, a bathroom, or even a mudroom! If they personalize their own place to hang their coats and backpacks, perhaps they will even be more inclined to hang up their things. One can dream, right?

What You'll Need:

- ○ 1 piece of pine measuring 11" × 7¼" × ¾"
- ○ Tape measure
- ○ Pencil
- ○ Jigsaw with a 10 TPI (teeth per inch) blade meant for wood
- ○ Wood filler
- ○ Sandpaper (120, 150, 220 grit)
- ○ Tack cloth
- ○ 1 Shaker peg measuring 3½" long
- ○ Drill
- ○ ½" drill bit (The size of the bit will be determined by the size of the Shaker peg you use)
- ○ Wood glue
- ○ 1" painter's tape
- ○ Chalkboard paint (black and gray)
- ○ 2 1" foam paintbrushes
- ○ Steel sawtooth ring hanger (rated for at least 20 pounds)
- ○ Chalk

What You'll Do:

1. On your wood, mark out a square that measures 7¼" × 7¼" and a triangular roof on top of it that measures 7¼" × 3¾" high. Draw it using the pencil and a straight edge. If desired, make a rectangle chimney on top of the roof, measuring 1" × 1½".

2. Cut out the house shape as one piece with the jigsaw, staying just outside of your pencil line.

> *Note:* I used a jigsaw for this project, but a small handsaw and/or a coping saw could also work just fine, although the pieces may require more sanding.

3. Fill in any imperfections with wood filler.

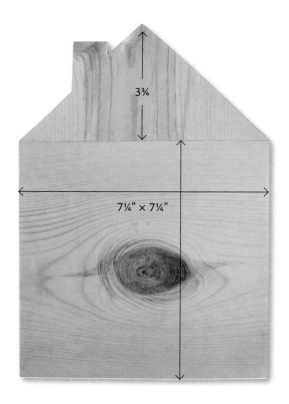

3¾

7¼" × 7¼"

4. Sand the top and sides of the work pieces until they are smooth. Begin with 120-grit sandpaper and work up to 220 grit if necessary. Clean up with tack cloth.

5. After the pieces have been sanded, mark the desired location of the Shaker peg.

6. Drill a ½"-wide hole, approximately ⅝" deep, to accommodate the end of the Shaker peg.

7. Dry fit and then install the peg using wood glue, making sure it is straight. Allow the wood glue to dry overnight.

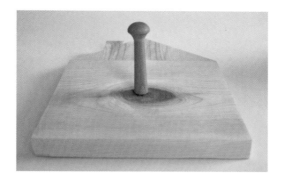

8. When the roof of the house has dried, apply painter's tape to the roof and paint the base of the house with 2–3 coats of the gray chalkboard paint. Remove the painter's tape when the paint has dried thoroughly.

9. Next, use painter's tape to tape off the roof section from the base of the house. Paint the roof of the house with 2–3 coats of the black chalkboard paint. Allow the paint to dry between coats and before removing the painter's tape.

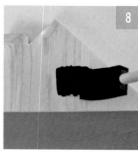

10. To hang your coat hook on the wall, install the steel sawtooth ring picture hanger (rated for 20 pounds) in the center of the house-shaped coat hook, following the directions on the package.

11. Season the chalkboard coat hook by rubbing it with a piece of chalk and then erasing it before allowing your little ones to personalize their own coat hooks.

12. Hang their masterpiece on the wall in their room or in your mudroom.

If you don't like the shape of this coat hook, feel free to substitute any simple shape you prefer, such as a star, flower, or fish.

ART CADDY

Help the little artist in your life stay organized with an art caddy. She can write her own labels on the chalkboard compartments, and it's just waiting to be filled with markers, crayons, scissors, and glue bottles. Even better, since the art caddy has a handle for those tiny hands, children will be able to tote their supplies around wherever they want. They never sit still for long, do they?

What You'll Need:

- Sides: 2 pieces of pine measuring 12" × 4" × ½"
- Ends: 2 pieces of pine measuring 8" × 5½" × ½"
- Bottom: 1 piece of pine measuring 11" × 5½" × ½"
- Handle: 1 piece of pine measuring 12" × 1½" × ½"
- Long divider: 1 piece of pine measuring 11" × 3½" × ¼"
- Short dividers: 2 pieces of pine measuring 5½" × 3½" × ¼"
- Table saw (A 12" compound miter saw or jigsaw could work depending on the size of the boards you begin with; handsaws could also work.)
- Tape measure
- Pencil
- Wood glue
- Brad nailer (or hammer with small nails)
- 1" brad nails
- Clamps
- Sandpaper (150, 220 grit)
- Wood filler

- Tack cloth
- White semigloss paint (or any color of your choice)
- Chalkboard paint

- 2 1" foam paintbrushes
- 1" painter's tape
- Chalk
- Chalk marker

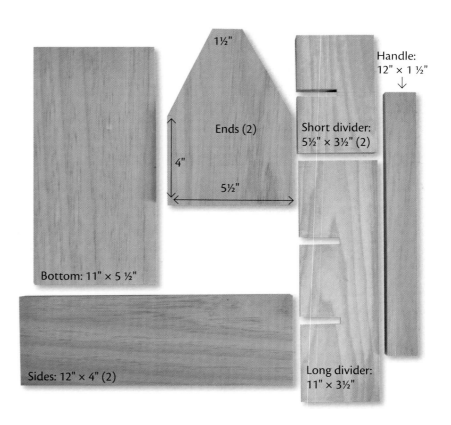

1½"

Ends (2)

4"

5½"

Bottom: 11" × 5 ½"

Sides: 12" × 4" (2)

Handle:
12" × 1 ½"
↓

Short divider:
5½" × 3½" (2)

Long divider:
11" × 3½"

What You'll Do:

1. Measure and cut your wood to the dimensions specified in the materials list, using the table saw.

2. To finish the end pieces, place them with the long sides vertical. Make a mark 4" from the bottom on both the left and right sides. Next, along the top of each end piece, measure 2" from each edge and make two additional marks. These should be 1½" apart and centered on the top of each end piece (this represents the location of the handle). Using a straight edge, connect each mark on the sides to the nearest mark on the top of the piece. Use the table saw (or miter saw or jigsaw) to cut along these lines. Do this on both end pieces.

3. To make sure everything fits together, dry fit all of the pieces. On a flat surface, lay the bottom piece down and set the sides and ends in place surrounding the bottom. Once everything has been checked for accuracy, glue the edges where they meet, clamp everything in place, and secure together, using 1" brad nails.

4. Glue and nail the handle in place using 1" brad nails.

5. Next, complete work on the ¼" pine dividers you cut earlier. Mark out the location of the small dividers along the long main divider that runs down the middle of the box. To do this, measure 3⅝" from each end and make a mark. Then, measure 3⅞" from each end and make another mark. This will give you the width of the two notches you will cut. Measure from the bottom of the divider 1¾" up and draw a line representing the depth of the cut. Remove the material at these two locations using the table saw or small handsaw, creating two notches that are each ¼" wide by 1¾" high.

6. For the two smaller dividers, measure from the end and make a mark at 2⅝" and 2⅞", checking from each end to make sure they are centered on the length of the board. Using the table saw or small handsaw, remove the material 1¾" up the height of the board at this location on both small dividers, creating a notch that is ¼" wide and 1¾" high, located in the middle of each small divider.

7. Slip the two small dividers into the notches on the long main divider and friction fit these pieces in place within the caddy. Don't glue them; a friction fit will allow you to remove these dividers at any time for cleaning or other maintenance.

8. With some 150-grit sandpaper, round over and soften any rough sides or edges.

9. Fill in any nail holes with wood filler and sand smooth with the 150-grit sandpaper, finishing with the 220 grit, if necessary.

10. Remove any dust and debris with a tack cloth.

11. After the art caddy is assembled and sanded, paint the entire art caddy with 1–2 coats of the white semigloss paint.

12. When the white paint has dried, tape off the top edge of the art caddy box and paint it with 2–3 coats of chalkboard paint. When the paint has dried, use the 1" painter's tape to protect any areas of the art caddy you wish to remain paint free. I chose to paint the two biggest sides of the art caddy.

13. When the chalkboard paint has dried, season it by rubbing it with a piece of chalk and then erasing it.

14. Have your child help fill each compartment with art supplies and label each section with the chalk marker.

You can use this caddy to organize things other than art supplies—for example, toy tools or hair accessories. You can also leave the dividers out and make your little handyman or handywoman a toolbox.

STEP STOOL

Please watch Your STEP!

My boys love to help me out in the kitchen when I am cooking or baking. However, they're still quite small, and reaching the countertops and the kitchen island can be difficult for them. This step stool is the perfect thing to have in the kitchen with little ones because it is sturdy, wide, and has a place for them to occupy themselves with doodling, in case there are one too many cooks in the kitchen!

What You'll Need:

- ○ Lower stair tread: 1 stair tread measuring 17½" × 6¾" × 1". (This is an actual stair tread, but the dimensions of the width and depth have been modified.)
- ○ Upper stair tread: 1 stair tread measuring 17½" × 10 ¾" × 1". (This is an actual stair tread, but the dimensions of the width and depth have been modified.)
- ○ Small box front and back: 2 pieces of ¾" pine measuring 16" × 6"
- ○ Small box sides: 2 pieces of ¾" pine measuring 6" × 6"
- ○ Large box front and back: 2 pieces of ¾" pine measuring 14½" × 13"
- ○ Large box sides: 2 pieces of ¾" pine measuring 10" × 13"
- ○ Tape measure
- ○ Pencil

- ○ Kreg pocket screw jig system (including pocket hole drill guide, ⅜" stepped drill bit with depth collar, and #2 square driver). You can use any Kreg pocket screw jig system for any of the projects in this book. They all work the same way and accomplish the same thing.
- ○ 80 1¼" coarse-thread stainless steel pocket screws
- ○ 10 1¼" wood screws
- ○ Clamps
- ○ Wood glue
- ○ Wood filler
- ○ Sandpaper (120, 150, 220 grit)
- ○ Tack cloth
- ○ White semigloss paint
- ○ Chalkboard paint
- ○ 1" foam paintbrush
- ○ 2" bristle paintbrush
- ○ Chalk

Note: Pocket holes are drilled into one piece of wood at an angle. That piece is then joined to a second piece, using self-tapping pocket screws. The screw jig system that I've included in the equipment list (and in the lists for other projects) should help you to drill pocket holes in this and other projects where they're called for.

What You'll Do:

1. Using the pocket hole jig system, drill pocket holes on the inside of the front and back of the small box on both ends to secure the sides of the box together. Drill additional pocket holes on the top of the front and back sides and at the top of the 6" sides to secure the stair tread later. For this box, pocket holes were always drilled in pairs of two approximately 6" apart.

2. Construct the small box, positioning the front and back (16" × 6") between the two sides (6" × 6"). Glue the edges where they meet and clamp them together. Secure the sides together using 1¼" pocket screws.

3. Again, using the pocket hole jig system, drill pocket holes on the inside of the front and back of the large box on both ends to secure the sides of the box together. Drill additional pocket holes on the top of the front and back sides and at the top of the 10" sides to secure the stair tread later. Again for this box, pocket holes were always drilled in pairs of two approximately 6" apart.

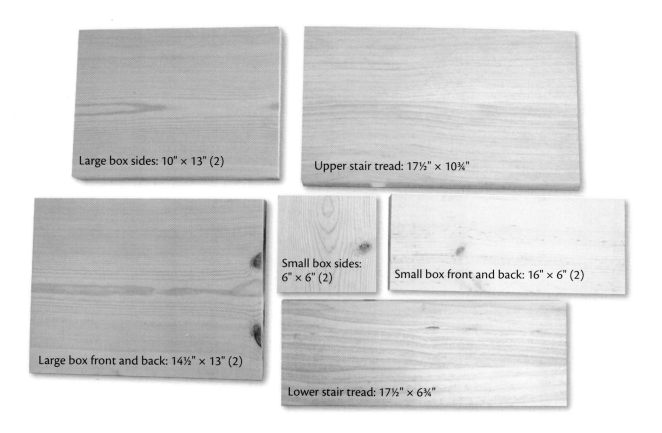

Large box sides: 10" × 13" (2)

Upper stair tread: 17½" × 10¾"

Small box sides: 6" × 6" (2)

Small box front and back: 16" × 6" (2)

Large box front and back: 14½" × 13" (2)

Lower stair tread: 17½" × 6¾"

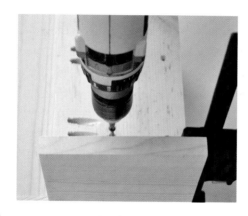

4. Construct the large box, positioning the front and back (14½" wide × 13" high) between the two sides (10" wide × 13" high). Glue the edges where they meet and clamp them together. Secure using 1¼" pocket screws.

5. Begin by laying the back box right side up. Place the smaller box right side up in front of the back box, making sure the ends are even. Secure both boxes together using wood glue and 1¼" wood screws. Space the screws evenly in two rows.

6. Center the lower stair tread (17½" × 6¾") on the small box. Secure from underneath using 1¼" pocket screws in the pocket screw holes you drilled earlier.

7. Center the upper stair tread (17½" × 10¾") on the large box. Secure from underneath using 1¼" pocket screws in the pocket screw holes you drilled earlier.

8. Fill all screw holes and imperfections in the wood with the wood filler and allow it to dry. Sand all edges and surfaces of the stool with the sandpaper, beginning with the 120 grit and ending with the 220 grit. Remove any dust and debris using the tack cloth.

9. Using the bristle paintbrush, paint the entire stool with 2–3 coats of the white semigloss paint. Be sure to read the manufacturer's instructions on the label for drying times in between each coat of paint. Allow the final coat of paint to dry overnight.

10. When the white paint has dried, paint 2–3 coats of chalkboard paint on both the lower and upper vertical risers of the step stool.

11. Season the chalkboard risers on the stool by rubbing them with a piece of chalk and then erasing them. You are now ready to use your chalkboard stool.

You can use this stool not only in the kitchen, but anywhere a child might need some help reaching things, such as in a bathroom, bedroom, or closet. Who says this stool is just for children though? Use it yourself to help you reach those upper cabinets or as a stand on which to set potted plants. The possibilities are endless.

PULL TOY

All little kids seem to love pulling something behind them as they walk along. Pull toys can even help develop coordination and balance. Why not make your own pull toy for the special little one in your life? Since this pull toy is in the form of a little wagon, your child can pull around his or her favorite toys and stuffed animals wherever he or she goes.

What You'll Need:

- Bottom: 1 piece of pine measuring 12" × 8" × ¾"
- Front and back: 2 pieces of pine measuring 8" × 2" × ½"
- Sides: 2 pieces of pine measuring 13" × 2" × ½"
- Wheels: 1 piece of pine measuring 5" × 5" × ¾"
- Axle enclosure: 4 pieces of pine measuring ½" × 8" × ¾"
- Axle enclosure top: 2 pieces of pine measuring 8" × 1⅛" × ¼"
- Axle: 2 ½" oak dowels measuring 10"
- Tape measure
- Pencil
- Table saw or circular saw
- Wood glue
- Clamps
- Brad nailer (or hammer and nails)
- 1¼" brad nails
- ¾" brad nails
- Drill
- Hole saw: 2⅛"
- Drill bits: ½", ⅛"
- Wood filler
- Sandpaper (120, 150, 220 grit)

- Tack cloth
- White semigloss paint
- 1" painter's tape
- Chalkboard paint

- 2 1" foam paintbrushes
- Chalk
- String measuring 36"
- ½" wooden bead

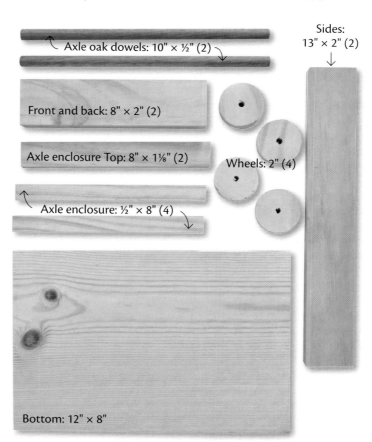

Axle oak dowels: 10" × ½" (2)

Sides: 13" × 2" (2)

Front and back: 8" × 2" (2)

Axle enclosure Top: 8" × 1⅛" (2)

Wheels: 2" (4)

Axle enclosure: ½" × 8" (4)

Bottom: 12" × 8"

What You'll Do:

1. Cut the wood to the measurements specified in the list.

2. Dry fit the pieces. Lay the 12" × 8" bottom piece on a flat work surface. Position the front and back (each 8" × 2") and two sides (each 13" × 2") in place around the bottom. Once everything has been checked for a tight fit, glue the edges where the pieces meet and clamp the pieces together. Secure using 1¼" brad nails.

3. Next, flip the work piece over. Run a bead of glue on the ½" side of the axle enclosure and position it ½" from the end and sides. Using 1¼" brad nails, nail it in place. Then set the oak dowel next to it to act as a spacer. Be sure the dowel spins freely before gluing and nailing the second axle enclosure piece down. Once the position has been checked, glue and nail the second axle support piece in place using wood glue and 1¼" brad nails. Repeat this process on the other end for the second set of

axle supports. Finally, attach the 8" × 1⅛" pine axle enclosure top to the top of each axle support section using wood glue and ¾" brad nails.

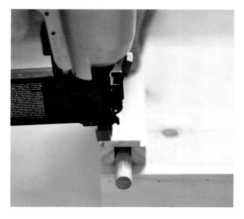

4. To make the wheels, take the piece of ¾" pine and drill four holes using the 2⅛" hole saw and drill. Each wheel will be 2" in diameter. Using wood filler, on each wheel fill in the hole from the drill bit on the side you would like facing out. On the other side of each wheel, enlarge the existing hole with the ½" drill bit, making it approximately ½" deep. This is where the axles will attach to the wheels.

5. Using the sandpaper, sand the wheels and the rest of the piece, beginning with the 120-grit sandpaper and working up to the 220 grit if necessary. Wipe up any dust and debris with the tack cloth.

6. Paint the inside and bottom of the wagon with 2–3 coats of the white semigloss paint. Allow the final coat of paint to dry overnight.

7. Use the painter's tape to tape off any portions of the wagon you wish to remain white.

8. Paint the outside of the wagon and the wheels with 2–3 coats of chalkboard paint. Read the manufacturer's instructions on the label of your chalkboard paint for drying times between each coat.

9. Once the paint has dried, slide the 10" oak dowel through the axle support and attach the wheels to the axle, using wood glue. Repeat this process on the other end of the wagon.

10. Season the chalkboard portion of the pull toy by rubbing it with a piece of chalk and then erasing it.

11. Attach the string by first drilling a ⅛" hole in the middle of the front side of the wagon. Slide the string through the hole and tie a knot on the inside, holding it in place. Attach the bead to the other end, using glue to hold it in place. You can also knot the end of the string to make the bead more secure.

If you chose to make this pull toy for a baby who can't quite walk yet, feel free to leave the string and bead off of the toy. The child will be able to push it around in a seated or crawling position. If using the string and wooden bead, **always ensure the child is under proper supervision** when using this toy, as the string and bead can pose a possible strangulation/choking hazard.

Shadow Box

I think art in a child's room or playroom should be meaningful and important to him or her. But, as you probably know, children change interests frequently—sometimes, it seems, about every 10 minutes. Because of that, this chalkboard shadow box is perfect for them. They can change it whenever the mood strikes them—fill it with cool superheroes one week and their favorite work of art the next. The chalkboard background makes it easily customizable; they can write whatever they like on it. When doing this project with my son, we chose to commemorate the completion of his first year of kindergarten. We filled the shadow box with some favorite art projects and examples of his writing, and we wrote his likes and dislikes on the chalkboard background. Let the children in your life fill it with whatever they like and display it proudly!

What You'll Need:

- ○ Shadow box purchased online, at any craft store, department store, or large chain store
- ○ 1" foam paintbrush
- ○ Green chalkboard paint
- ○ Chalk
- ○ Items to place in your shadow box (to be determined by you)

What You'll Do:

1. You will need to disassemble the shadow box. Remove the back portion from the frame and glass and set the frame and glass aside. If necessary, wash the glass portion of the shadow box and allow it to dry thoroughly.

2. Using the 1" foam paintbrush, paint a couple of coats of the chalkboard paint on the back of the shadow box. Be sure to read the manufacturer's instructions on the label for drying times in between each coat of paint.

3. Once the paint has dried, rub the surface of the chalkboard paint with a piece of white chalk and then erase it. You are now ready to fill your shadow box with various items and write on the chalkboard background.

You don't need to confine this project to your child's bedroom or playroom. Why not have a collection of shadow boxes and fill them with memories, pictures, and souvenirs from each family vacation? Choose a chalkboard paint color that suits your style and then write where and when you vacationed on the chalkboard portion. You can include a family picture as well as some seashells you found on your beach vacation. If you are a parent or grandparent, designate a shadow box for each child or grandchild. Write his or her name, birth date, or a favorite funny quote from when he or she was little on the chalkboard portion. The shadow box can be filled with pictures and special mementos from each child. Or, change the shadow box for each season or holiday. Write the lyrics to a favorite Christmas carol on the chalkboard and fill with a few of your favorite yuletide ornaments, a few pinecones, or a sprig of holly.

LUNCHBOX

When I was little, there was nothing I liked better than getting a note from my mom in my lunchbox at school. It made me a little less homesick during a long day. Do the same thing for your little ones, but instead of using a piece of paper and a pen, use a chalkboard and a piece of chalk. Maybe your child will even be inspired to do a little writing of his own and impress the teacher!

What You'll Need:

- ○ Metal lunchbox
- ○ 1" painter's tape
- ○ Garbage bag
- ○ Primer spray paint (for metal)
- ○ Chalkboard spray paint
- ○ Chalk

What You'll Do:

1. Wash and dry the lunchbox thoroughly.

2. Using the painter's tape, block off any portions of the lid on the lunchbox you wish to remain paint free. Place the box portion of the lunchbox into the garbage bag, leaving the lid/cover out. Use painter's tape to hold the bag in place. This will allow you to paint the lid/cover but keep the remainder of the lunchbox paint free.

3. In a well-ventilated area, spray 1–2 thin coats of the primer spray paint. Be sure to read the manufacturer's instructions on the label for drying times in between each coat of paint.

4. After the primer has dried, spray the unblocked areas of the lunchbox with 2–3 thin coats of the chalkboard spray paint. Be sure to read the label for drying times in between each coat of paint.

5. After the final coat of paint has dried, season the chalkboard surface by rubbing it with a piece of chalk and erasing it.

You are ready to send a note, a reminder, or a funny joke to school with your little ones to make them smile. Now, if only there were a way to see their reactions as they read your notes every day.

> *Note:* I recommend that you hand wash this metal lunchbox.

CLOCK

Learning how to tell time on a clock can be a tricky concept for a child to master (sometimes it's a little difficult for adults to get our heads around). By painting an ordinary clock with some chalkboard paint, you will be able to introduce even the smallest child to telling time. When they're little, include some simple pictures, such as a book, bed, or food, next to the numbers or in place of the numbers. Place the clock in a spot where you can refer to it at important times during the day, such as lunchtime, bath time, and bedtime. As children get older, you can replace the pictures with numbers and even have them write in the numbers. Roman numerals or simple math problems involving time are appropriate for older children. Whatever you or your children decide to write on your chalkboard clock, it will be time well spent!

What You'll Need:

- ○ An inexpensive wall clock
- ○ 1" painter's tape
- ○ Chalkboard paint
- ○ 1" foam paintbrush
- ○ Chalk

What You'll Do:

1. Remove the plastic cover on the wall clock.

2. With the painter's tape, block off any portions of the clock that you don't want covered with chalkboard paint, such as the hands and clock base.

3. Using the 1" foam paintbrush, paint a couple of coats of the chalkboard paint on the face of the clock. Be sure to read the manufacturer's instructions on the label for drying times in between each coat of paint.

4. Once the paint has dried, rub the surface of the chalkboard paint with a piece of white chalk and then erase it. You are now ready to write on your chalkboard clock.

Display the clock in a place where your children will see it often, such as a bedroom, playroom, or family room.

CHAPTER FOUR

Celebratory Creations

Everyone loves a good party, whether it's big or small. It may be the guest list that makes any celebration a good one, but a tasty menu, some festive decorations, and useful props can turn a good party into something fabulous. Take off some of the pressure by doing chalkboard party projects ahead of time, personalizing them, and using them again and again. Wow your guests with your rustic menu cards, a cake topper, or a beer-tasting tray. This chapter also includes projects such as chargers, napkin rings, and chevron votive holders that you can use both at celebrations and every day.

Cake Silhouette Table Runner

Birthdays are one of the highlights of family life. Because this table runner can be customized and reused, it can take some of the stress out of decorating for every birthday celebration.

What You'll Need:

- Plain table runner, in the color of your choice
- 1 sheet of heavy card stock
- Pencil
- Scissors or craft knife
- Ruler
- Piece of cardboard
- 1" painter's tape (optional)
- Bottle of multisurface chalkboard paint
- 1" foam paintbrush
- Chalk

What You'll Do:

1. Wash and dry your table runner according to the manufacturer's instructions.

2. Draw a simple picture onto the piece of card stock. This will become your silhouette. I chose to draw a simple cupcake with a candle on the top. Some appropriate party pictures might be a cupcake, a present, a balloon, or a cake on a cake stand. Carefully cut out the picture, using the scissors or craft knife.

3. Place the cut card stock silhouette onto the end of the table runner, using the ruler to make sure it is centered and straight. Using the pencil, trace the outline of the silhouette onto the table runner.

4. Place the cardboard underneath the area that you will paint in order to protect your work surface because paint will most likely leak through to the other side of the table runner.

5. Using the foam paintbrush, carefully paint with the chalkboard paint on the inside of the traced area. If you think you might have difficulty staying in the lines, apply painter's tape to the outline of the project. Take care to not get the paint too thick near the painter's tape in case it begins to bleed through the fabric underneath the tape. This project will require approximately 2–3 coats of paint. Be sure to read the manufacturer's instructions on the label for drying times in between each coat of paint.

6. After the chalkboard paint has dried, rub the entire chalk surface with a piece of chalk and then erase it. You are now ready to write on your chalkboard silhouette table runner.

Note: I recommend that you spot treat this table runner to protect the painted portion. If washing is necessary, hand wash the table runner in cold water; don't run it through a washer or dryer.

As long as we are celebrating, why not use this table runner for an anniversary party or a baby shower? Who says cake is just for birthdays?

Faux-Slate Serving Tray

It seems like people featured in fancy magazines are always using slate serving trays and pieces to serve food at functions. However, buying a piece of slate for this purpose can be expensive for the rest of us, especially if you would like more than one serving tray. This faux-slate serving tray looks and acts just like the real thing, but at a fraction of the cost and weight. Not only that, but this project could not be easier to complete.

What You'll Need:

- ○ ¼" × 14½" × 6¾" piece of plywood sanded on two sides (modify size to meet your needs)
- ○ Oscillating multitool (such as the Rockwell Sonicrafter) fitted with an HSS 3⅛" semicircle saw blade (or similar blade, depending on brand)
- ○ Sandpaper (150 grit)
- ○ Tack cloth
- ○ Chalkboard paint
- ○ 1" foam paintbrush
- ○ Chalk

What You'll Do:

1. Use the multitool with a 3⅛" semicircle saw blade to gently remove the edge of the plywood. Hold the blade at various angles to the work piece and gently shave off material until you achieve the layered look of slate. Extend this process in about ¼" from the edge of the work piece. Do this to all four sides. Once complete, flip the piece over and repeat the process on the other side. Remember, you can always take more material off, so begin slowly, work on both sides, and examine your work frequently.

2. Using 150-grit sandpaper, sand the entire piece. Hand sanding works best here because there is not much material to remove and it is easier to control than a power tool. You do not want to destroy the fine slate-like edge you just crafted.

3. Clean up any dust and debris from the piece with the tack cloth before painting.

4. Using the foam paintbrush, cover the front, back, and edges with 2–3 coats of chalkboard paint. Be sure to read the manufacturer's instructions on the label for drying times between each coat of paint.

5. Once the paint has dried, season the entire piece by rubbing it with chalk and then erasing it.

You are now ready to use your faux-slate serving tray. Use this serving tray to display fine cheeses or create your own antipasti platter.

Note: It is recommended that you not place food directly onto the serving tray. Using parchment, wax, or brown paper underneath will protect the surface of the tray as well as prevent any ingestion of paint.

RUSTIC-WOOD MENU CARD

Menu cards can class up a dinner party like nothing else. At your next party or get-together, why not display your menu so that your guests will know what they will be eating? Simple touches like this will make people feel comfortable, special, and welcome at your house.

What You'll Need:

- Piece of 5" × 3" × ¼" plywood
- Saw (handsaw, miter saw, or table saw)
- Measuring tape
- Sandpaper (150, 220 grit)
- Chalkboard paint
- 1" foam paintbrush
- Chalk
- Small wooden stump, cut from a fallen tree branch, measuring roughly 1½" × 2½"

What You'll Do:

1. Using the saw and measuring tape, measure and cut the plywood to the dimensions specified.

2. Using the fine-grit sandpaper, gently sand away any rough spots and rough edges from the plywood.

3. Using the paintbrush, paint a couple of coats of chalkboard paint on all sides of the plywood. Be sure to read the manufacturer's instructions on the label for drying times in between each coat of paint.

4. After the paint has dried, season the plywood by rubbing a piece of chalk over the entire surface and then erasing it.

5. In the middle of one of the flat sides of the wooden stump, cut a notch ¼" deep and ¼" wide in the top big enough to allow the ¼" plywood to fit securely inside.

You are now ready to write your menu for your party and display it for your guests. The best part about this project is that this menu card can be used many times for any function. Why not make a bunch and send a menu card home with each one of your guests as a parting gift? Instead of using it as a menu card, you could write his or her name on it and use it as a place card in your table setting. Simple, yet thoughtful touches such as these will make your guests look forward to coming again!

CHARGER

Chargers are something else that can make your table setting look fancy. Painting a plain, inexpensive charger with chalkboard paint will allow you to use it for many things: a place card, a menu board, or even just a simple greeting to your guests. Feel free to use any type or color of charger for this project. I chose to use wood, since I know that it will pair well with almost any table setting and can be used during all four seasons.

What You'll Need:

- ○ Wooden charger
- ○ Painter's tape (optional)
- ○ Chalkboard paint
- ○ 1" foam paintbrush
- ○ Chalk

What You'll Do:

1. Tape off any portions of your charger that you wish to remain free of paint.

2. Paint the charger with 2–3 coats of chalkboard paint. Be sure to read the manufacturer's instructions on the label for drying times in between each coat of paint.

3. When the paint has dried, season the charger by rubbing it with a piece of chalk and then erasing it.

You are now ready to write on your chalkboard charger.

Beverage Centerpiece

Here's an idea for your next party that will make bartending simple (not to mention a bit cheaper). Choose a base cocktail that you'll serve all your guests—but one they can customize to suit their tastes. Then serve the customizing ingredients on this fancy-looking chalkboard centerpiece.

What You'll Need:

- Lazy Susan
- 1" painter's tape
- Chalkboard paint
- 1" foam paintbrush
- Chalk
- Items to place on your centerpiece, such as serving bowls filled with lemons, limes, and herbs, as well as bitters, spirits, ice, recipe options, etc.

What You'll Do:

1. Tape off any portions of the Lazy Susan that you do not want covered in chalkboard paint.

2. Using the foam paintbrush, paint 2–3 coats of chalkboard paint on the top of the Lazy Susan. Be sure to read the manufacturer's instructions on the label for drying times in between each coat of paint.

3. Once the paint has dried, season the chalkboard portion of the Lazy Susan by rubbing it with a piece of chalk and then erasing it.

You are now ready to fill the Lazy Susan with everything you need to stock your bar. Label the ingredients you have set out on the top of the Lazy Susan, or write out numbered steps for building a special cocktail.

Place the Lazy Susan in the center of your table and surround it with everything else you will need at your party: glassware, appetizers, and tableware.

Napkin Ring

Nothing sets the mood at a dinner party quite like a table set with the finest décor. Whether it is an intimate dinner for two or an elaborate dinner for twelve, raise your next gathering to a new level with chalkboard napkin rings. An added bonus to this project? These napkin rings can also serve as table setting markers, accomplishing two goals at once and making throwing a dinner party that much easier, whatever the number of guests!

What You'll Need:

- ○ Napkin rings (should have a surface that can be written on)
- ○ Painter's tape (optional; size dependent on the size of the napkin rings)
- ○ Chalkboard spray paint
- ○ Chalk

What You'll Do:

1. Tape off any portions of each napkin ring that you wish to remain free of paint.

2. In a well-ventilated area, spray each napkin ring with 2–3 thin coats of the chalkboard spray paint. Be sure to read the manufacturer's instructions on the label for drying times in between each coat of paint.

3. Once the paint has dried, season each napkin ring by rubbing it with a piece of chalk and then erasing it.

You are now ready to write on your chalkboard napkin ring.

If your party has a distinct color theme, using a matching or complementary color of chalkboard paint would be even more impressive!

CAKE TOPPERS

Cake toppers are popular at birthday parties, and I think we all know why. They can take an ordinary cake and make it that much more festive. Impress the guests at your next party by making these chalkboard cake toppers yourself! The best thing about them is that since they're covered with chalkboard paint, you can customize them for any occasion and use them again and again.

What You'll Need:

- ○ 4 wood craft circles (number dependent on what you would like your cake topper to say)
- ○ 2 ⅛" wooden skewers 8½" long
- ○ Drill
- ○ ⅛" brad point drill bit (the size of your wooden skewer)
- ○ Chalkboard paint
- ○ 1" foam paintbrush
- ○ Scissors or cutters (to snip the skewers with)
- ○ Chalk

What You'll Do:

1. Drill a small hole centered anywhere on the lateral side of each wooden craft circle with the drill and ⅛" brad point drill bit. The hole should allow a wooden skewer to fit snugly inside.

Note: **A brad point drill bit works well on small pieces like this to keep the bit from slipping.**

2. Once the holes have been drilled, paint 2–3 coats of chalkboard paint on both sides and the edge of each craft circle. Be sure to read the manufacturer's instructions on the label for drying times in between each coat of paint.

3. Once the paint has dried, season the surface of each circle by rubbing it with a piece of chalk and erasing it.

4. Next, take the wooden skewers and carefully cut them in half. Insert the skewers into the painted craft circles.

You are now ready to place your cake toppers on top of your cake. You can write or draw anything you like on them. I chose to write "Happy Birthday to You" on mine, which is why I made four of them.

Get creative with your cake topper. If your party has a color theme, purchase chalkboard paint in those colors. Use colorful chalk or chalkboard pens for even more festive fun. Or, make them in a smaller size for darling cupcake toppers! Happy celebrating!

BEER-SERVING PADDLE

Why not make several of these beer-serving paddles to use at your own craft beer-tasting party? This beer-serving paddle has **4** helpful holes for glasses, so your guests will be able to taste and enjoy **4** different beers. The chalkboard portion of the paddle will allow you to write down which beers are being tasted and is the perfect place for your guests to record their favorite beer on the paddle. The convenient handle makes the paddle easier to hold on to when carried.

What You'll Need:

- ○ Piece of pine measuring 16" × 7¼" × ¾" before the handle is formed
- ○ Piece of ¼" plywood to be used as a template, measuring at least 14" × 4½" for stability (This is not necessary if you use a Forstner drill bit to make the holes.)
- ○ Tape measure
- ○ Pencil
- ○ Jigsaw fitted with a 10 TPI blade meant for wood
- ○ Drill
- ○ Hole saw: 2⅛" (This hole saw works for a glass with a bottom diameter of 2"; not all glass sizes are the same, so adjust your hole saw size accordingly.)
- ○ Plunge router
- ○ ½" straight bit for router
- ○ Template guide for router
- ○ 2" Forstner drill bit (only needed if not using router)
- ○ Wood filler (optional)
- ○ Clamps
- ○ Sandpaper (150, 220 grit)
- ○ Tack cloth
- ○ WATCO Danish Oil
- ○ Cheesecloth
- ○ Painter's tape (any size will do)
- ○ Chalkboard paint
- ○ 1" foam paintbrush
- ○ Chalk

circles: 2⅛"

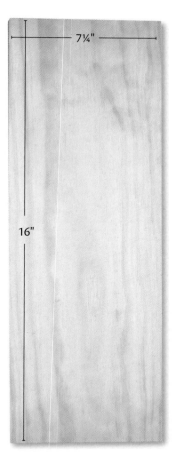

7¼"

16"

What You'll Do:

1. Begin by making a template for your router. Take a piece of ¼" plywood measuring a minimum of 14" × 4½" to a maximum of 16" × 7¼" and draw a line down the middle lengthwise. This will serve as a layout line for the holes you will drill as well as help you align it on the final piece. Mark the center of each of the four holes approximately 3" apart from one another (depending on the size of your glass). Using a 2⅛" hole saw, drill 4 holes at the marked locations. Your template is now complete. The holes in the template should be bigger that the bottom width of your tasting glasses, to account for the width of the guide piece on the router

2. Next, cut your ¾" piece of pine (or wood of your choice) 16" long. This will be the finished length of the paddle, but you'll remove some material to reveal the handle.

3. Draw a line down the middle of the board lengthwise. This will be used along with the line on the wood template to lay out the position of the holes on the finished piece.

4. Determine the position of the first hole from the end of the board. Using the ¼" plywood template, match up the layout lines on the template with those on the ¾" piece. Clamp the template securely to the piece and to a workbench.

5. Using a plunge router fitted with a template guide and a ½" straight bit, set the depth to ⅜". The final hole size is dependent upon the bottom diam-

eter of the glass you choose. Carefully remove the material within the circle using the router. Repeat this process for the three remaining holes.

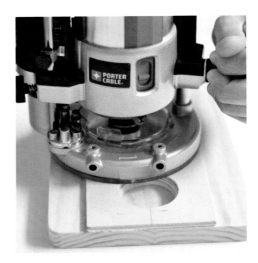

Note: **If you do not have access to a router or would prefer not to use one, you can also use a 2" Forstner bit to drill the 4 holes. Using this method will leave a small hole at the bottom of the circle in the middle, which can be left open or filled in with stainable wood filler.**

6. Next, copy the handle template from the Appendix. Cut out the paper template and lay it on the open end of the board. Trace around the template using a pencil. Remove the paper template from the wood. On the end opposite of the handle, draw a small curve near each corner to round and soften the edges. Once you are satisfied with the lines you drew, you are ready to begin cutting.

7. Clamp the board firmly in place to your work surface. Using a jigsaw, cut on the outside of your pencil mark revealing the handle with its round end and gracious curve. Cut also the two small curves on the other end.

8. Using the 150-grit sandpaper, round over all edges of the serving paddle, giving it a smooth feel. Finish sanding with the 220-grit sandpaper, being sure not to forget about the 4 holes you routed or drilled out.

9. Remove any additional dust and debris using a tack cloth. Apply your desired finish, using the cheesecloth. For this project, I recommend WATCO Danish Oil. Apply following manufacturer's directions. This type of finish is easy to apply and does not need any other protective finish unless you want it. For example, you could follow it up with clear satin polyurethane. Be sure to read the manufacturer's instructions on the label for drying times between each coat of finish.

10. Once the stain has dried thoroughly according the manufacturer's instructions on the label, use the painter's tape to mark off a large rectangle (or four small rectangles if you prefer) directly underneath the circles. This will be the area where you will apply the chalkboard paint.

11. Using the foam paintbrush, apply 2–3 coats of chalkboard paint to the inside of the taped-off area on the tasting tray. Be sure to read the manufacturer's instructions on the label for drying times between each coat of paint.

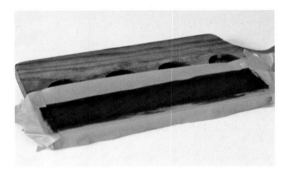

12. Season the chalkboard portion of the beer paddle by rubbing it with a piece of chalk and then erasing it.

You are now ready to use your beer-serving paddle. This serving paddle is, of course, not limited only to beers. It will work for any beverage tasting. For example, the 2" holes are large enough to accommodate the Glencairn Glass for a whiskey taste test. You can even include children and taste test different types of root beer. Cheers!

CHEVRON VOTIVE HOLDERS

Candles can be the perfect addition to any party and will give your home a warm, cozy atmosphere. These chevron votive holders will bring a bit of flair to any ordinary glass votive holder. Adding the chalkboard element to them will allow you to personalize them even further.

What You'll Need:

- ○ 4 glass votive holders
- ○ Pencil
- ○ Ruler
- ○ Scissors or craft knife
- ○ 1"–2" painter's tape
- ○ Chalkboard paint
- ○ 1" foam paintbrush
- ○ Chalk
- ○ Battery-operated LED tea lights

What You'll Do:

1. Unroll a piece of painter's tape big enough to go around the circumference of your votive holder. Use the pencil and ruler to draw the chevron patterns on a piece of painter's tape, using the pictures on the previous page to serve as a guide.

2. Carefully cut out the chevron patterns with the scissors. If using a craft knife, be sure to protect your work surface in order to prevent any damage to it.

3. Apply the chevron-patterned painter's tape to the votive holders. Take care to press the painter's tape down firmly to prevent any paint from leaking under it.

4. Apply 3–4 coats of chalkboard paint to the votive holder using the foam paintbrush. You will want to make sure that you cannot see any streaks or gaps in the chalkboard paint, especially because there will be light shining behind it. Be sure to read the manufacturer's instructions on the label for drying times in between each coat of paint.

5. Once the paint has dried, carefully remove the painter's tape to reveal your chevron pattern.

6. Season the votive holder with a piece of chalk and then erase it. You are now ready to write on your little chevron chalkboard.

Note: I recommend that you use battery-operated tea lights inside of this votive holder. If you use real tea-light candles, do not leave them unattended and extinguish them once they begin to burn too low.

Displaying a number of these votive holders along with some flower arrangements down the length of your table can create a stunning effect at a party, bridal shower, or wedding.

CHAPTER FIVE

Outdoor Undertakings

Why confine your chalkboard projects to the indoors? They can be just as useful and beautiful outside. Of course, you will have to deal with the elements, mainly rain. However, don't let that stop you! Using a chalk marker will enable your writing to linger a bit longer than just a regular piece of chalk. Also, many of the projects—such as the paint-dipped flowerpots, the plant markers, and the toy and tool storage—can be done in a four-seasons porch, a front porch, the garage, or your patio. Go ahead, because isn't half the fun of a chalkboard being able to erase it and start again fresh?

PAINT-DIPPED FLOWERPOT

Take an ordinary household object—and what's more ordinary than a flowerpot—dip it in a little chalkboard paint, then transform your home, deck, or patio. It takes a bit of time and patience, but this project is an easy and fun one that you are sure to enjoy.

What You'll Need:

- ○ Flowerpot
- ○ Bucket (an old ice cream bucket works well)
- ○ Newspaper
- ○ 1"–2" painter's tape
- ○ Chalkboard paint
- ○ Chalk
- ○ Chalk marker

What You'll Do:

1. Wash and dry the flowerpot thoroughly.

2. Protect your work surface by laying down some newspaper. To prevent any paint from leaking through the hole at the bottom of the flowerpot, tape off the hole with some painter's tape.

3. Pour a small amount of paint into a bucket large enough for the flowerpot to fit into.

4. Carefully push the bottom (about a ½" of the actual pot) of the flowerpot into the paint. Then, carefully lift it out of the paint. This is where you will need to be very patient. Hold the flowerpot over the bucket and allow as much paint to drip off the bottom as possible. There will be more paint on there than you might think. Letting the paint drip off the bottom of the flowerpot will prevent the paint from running too much, which could create a mess on your work surface.

5. Once enough paint has dripped off the flowerpot, turn it upside down. The leftover paint on the flowerpot will slowly drip down toward the top and leave you with a pretty paint-dipped effect. Dipping the pot into the paint will give you a thick coat of paint, so repeating the process is not necessary.

6. Allow the chalkboard paint to dry for 24 hours before seasoning it with a piece of chalk. By writing with a chalk marker, anything that you write or draw on the flowerpots will last a little bit longer.

Use paint-dipped chalkboard flowerpots to label your flowers, herbs, container vegetables, or to keep track of your plant-watering schedule for delicate plants. Make some for your friends or family and write a sweet sentiment on the flowerpot—a gift they are sure to enjoy.

> *Note:* If the drip look of these pots isn't your style, you can always dip them and let them dry without flipping them over.

PLANT MARKERS

Keep track of the types of herbs, vegetables, or flowers in your garden or flowerpots with these plant markers. By using chalkboard paint and sturdy composite shims, which will not rot like wood, you can use these plant markers in your garden for many years to come. Don't forget to use a chalk marker, which will not be permanent but will hold up to rain or water much better than regular chalk.

What You'll Need:

- ○ Composite shims, found at any building supply or hardware store or online
- ○ Primer spray paint
- ○ Chalkboard spray paint
- ○ Chalk
- ○ Chalk marker

What You'll Do:

1. In a well-ventilated area, spray the sides and edges of each composite shim with 1–2 coats of the primer spray paint. Be sure to read the manufacturer's instructions on the label for drying times in between each coat of primer.

2. After the primer has dried, spray 2–3 coats of the chalkboard spray paint on the sides and edges of each composite shim. Be sure to read the manufacturer's instructions on the label for drying times in between each coat of paint.

3. After the paint has dried, season each composite shim by rubbing it with a piece of chalk and then erasing it.

4. Use the chalk marker to write the name of your plants on each plant marker and then place them in your garden or flowerpots. Remembering the names of those flowers, herbs, and vegetables has never been easier!

If you're like me and forgetful about when you last watered or fertilized a plant, why not write down the date each task was done? If you don't want to look at that information all the time, write it on the back, where you'll always know where to find it.

Barn Wood–Framed Outdoor Chalkboard

I love projects that use barn wood—the grain of the wood shows beautifully, and it has an attractive rustic feel. An outdoor chalkboard on your deck or patio might be just the thing where you can write down the menu for your next barbecue, play games, or keep score on family game night. Your children will enjoy having a space to color and draw. By making the chalkboard a manageable size, you can move it indoors during rainy days and in the winter to protect it from the elements.

What You'll Need:

- ○ Pine boards measuring 60" × 11¼" × ¾"

BARN WOOD FRAME PIECES:
- ○ Stiles/Vertical pieces: 60" x 2¼" (2)
- ○ Rails/Horizontal pieces: 18" x 2¼" (2)

> **Note:** Projects made from barn wood are growing in popularity. The result is that you can find it in a lot of places. Go online to Craigslist or some other site or check your local home improvement store. You can also hunt around farms (of course, with the permission of the owner). The owner may even have some old barn wood he's willing to give you or sell you cheap.

- ○ Tape measure
- ○ Pencil
- ○ Circular saw (or table saw or handsaw)

- ○ Drill
- ○ Kreg pocket screw jig system (including pocket hole drill guide, ⅜" stepped drill bit with depth collar, and #2 square driver)
- ○ Stainless steel pocket screws
- ○ Wood glue (exterior grade)
- ○ Clamps
- ○ Wood filler (exterior grade)

- ○ Nail gun (or hammer and nails)
- ○ 1¼" stainless steel brad nails
- ○ Sandpaper (150, 220 grit)
- ○ Primer (for wood)
- ○ Chalkboard paint
- ○ 2 2" foam paintbrushes or roller
- ○ Chalk

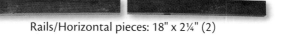

Rails/Horizontal pieces: 18" x 2¼" (2)

Stiles/Vertical pieces: 60" x 2¼" (2)

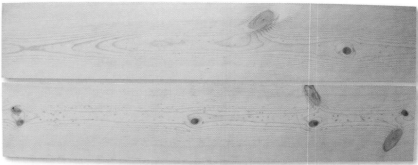

Pine boards measuring 60" × 11¼"

What You'll Do:

1. Using the pocket hole jig, drill two pocket holes at least every foot (or 1 every 6 inches) running the length of the boards.

2. To create the wood background, lay the pine boards side by side on a flat surface. Run a thin bead of exterior grade wood glue along the long edges where the pine boards will meet. Insert the screws into the pocket holes you drilled earlier on the back side. This makes for a quick and secure way to keep the boards together.

> *Note:* If you do not have a pocket screw jig, you could always use strips of ½" or ¾" wood on the back side of the boards running perpendicular to your main boards and either nail or screw them together.

3. To achieve a large flat surface, use exterior grade wood filler on the seam where the two boards meet. After the wood filler has set according to manufacturer's specifications, sand the seam flat using the 150-grit sandpaper, working up to the 220 grit as necessary.

4. Dry fit the frame pieces by laying them on top of the background. Locate the two 18" rail pieces between the two 60" stile pieces being sure the outside edges and joints line up correctly.

5. Once the wood background and frame have been checked for a proper fit, prime the background with 1–2 coats of the primer. Be sure to read the manufacturer's instructions on the label for drying times between each coat of primer.

6. When the primer has dried, paint the boards with 1–2 coats of the chalkboard paint. Be sure to read the manufacturer's instructions on the label for drying times between each coat of paint.

7. Once the chalkboard paint is dry, apply exterior grade wood glue to the location on the background where the frame will go (same as the dry fit).

8. Hold the frame tightly to the boards using clamps and attach the frame permanently, using 1¼" stainless steel brad nails.

9. Season the chalkboard by rubbing it with a piece of chalk and then erasing it.

10. It is likely that the surface of the old barn wood will be much darker than the new pine you used for the background and the cut sides of the barn wood. If this is the case, stain the sides of the pine and the cut sides of the barn wood to match the face of the barn wood trim you used. Follow manufacturer's directions on the stain you choose.

You are now ready to use your barn wood–framed outdoor chalkboard.

TOY STORAGE

Toys have an amazing habit of migrating. Put them on the patio at the end of the day and by the next afternoon they've all magically scattered themselves around the yard. Now you can keep them corralled with some chalkboard crates on wheels. You can easily label them on the chalkboard portion, which will help your children stay organized. You also have the flexibility to change what goes inside the crates as the kids' needs and interests change. The handy wheels make the crates easy to push around, allowing for easier cleanup and maneuverability. On your patio, porch, or even in the garage, the crates are a convenient and attractive way to store many toys.

What You'll Need:

- ○ 2 wooden crates
- ○ Primer spray paint (for wood)
- ○ Chalkboard spray paint
- ○ Drill
- ○ Drill bit (¼", size dependent on the screw on your wheels)
- ○ 8 1½" wheels and hardware for attaching them, found at any building supply or hardware store or the Internet
- ○ Chalk
- ○ Chalk marker

What You'll Do:

1. In a well-ventilated area, spray the inside and outside of each crate with 1–2 coats of primer. Be sure to read the manufacturer's instructions on the label for drying times in between each coat of primer.

2. Next, paint 3–4 coats of chalkboard spray paint to the inside and outside of each crate. Be sure to read the manufacturer's instructions on the label for drying times in between each coat of paint.

3. After the paint has dried, drill holes in each corner of both crates ¾" deep, but it will be dependent on the wheels you purchase.

4. Attach the wheels in each corner according to the directions on the package.

5. Season the outside of each crate by rubbing it with a piece of chalk and then erasing it.

Use the chalk marker to label each crate and then fill them up with your outdoor toys. Use these crates to organize anything, such as shoes and boots, mittens, or even board games!

Tape Measure with Chalk Holder

"Measure twice, cut once." This advice has been passed down from generation to generation because it's *good*. Yet somehow, I still find myself sometimes forgetting the measurements of the thing I just measured twice. So whether you are a perfectionist who wants to make sure you remember the exact dimensions of a piece before you make a cut, or you are just plain forgetful, this project will appeal to you. With this easy-to-make, convenient tape measure with a mini-chalkboard and chalk holder, you will not have to ask yourself, "Now what was that measurement?" Just write it down and carry it with you!

What You'll Need:

- ○ Tape measure
- ○ Painter's tape (optional)
- ○ Chalkboard paint
- ○ 1" foam paintbrush
- ○ Piece of leather measuring 4" × 1¼"
- ○ Chalk
- ○ Sewing/fabric scissors
- ○ Awl
- ○ Hammer
- ○ Screwdriver (Phillips)

What You'll Do:

1. Tape off any portions of the tape measure that you wish to remain free of paint.

2. Paint 2–3 coats of chalkboard paint onto one side of the tape measure enclosure. Be sure to read the manufacturer's instructions on the label for drying times in between each coat of paint.

3. While the paint on the tape measure is drying, mark out a 4" × 1¼" rectangle on the piece of leather, using the chalk.

4. Cut out the rectangle with the scissors. Again using the scissors, round over the corners.

5. Fold the leather in half and lay it next to the belt clip on the back side of the tape measure.

6. Using the chalk, mark the approximate location of the screw holding the belt clip in place on the leather.

7. Using an awl and hammer, pound a hole through both ends of the leather at the same time at the location you marked.

8. Remove the screw from the belt clip on the back of the tape measure using the screwdriver.

9. Slide the folded leather piece between the clip and reattach the screw through the holes you pounded through.

10. Season the chalkboard-painted portion of the tape measure with a piece of chalk and then erase it.

11. Slip your chalk through the loop. You now have a convenient way of remembering those tricky measurements.

This is a great learning tool for kids. Have them measure each other against a wall and then write down on the chalkboard surface the measurements in feet and inches. Ask them to measure other household items, write down their findings on the tape measure, and show it to you.

TOOL STORAGE

These sturdy metal pails are handy to have in your garden with you as you tend to your herbs, flowers, and vegetables. Use them to store your small shovels and trowels, fertilizer, or plant markers. Use the chalkboard-painted area on each pail to label each one, allowing you to find what you need quickly.

What You'll Need:

- ○ 3 galvanized metal pails
- ○ Primer spray paint (for metal)
- ○ Chalkboard spray paint
- ○ 1"–2" painter's tape
- ○ Garbage bags
- ○ Chalk
- ○ Chalk marker

What You'll Do:

1. Tape off the top two-thirds of each pail with the painter's tape, or wherever you wish to paint on your pails. To prevent any primer or chalkboard paint from getting on areas you wish to remain paint free, cover the remaining portions of the pails with the garbage bags and tape them into place.

2. In a well-ventilated area, spray 1–2 thin coats of the primer onto each pail. Be sure to read the label for drying times in between each coat of primer.

3. When the primer has dried, apply 2–3 thin coats of the chalkboard spray paint. Be sure to read the manufacturer's instructions on the label for drying times in between each coat of paint.

4. When the paint has dried, season each chalkboard portion of the pails by rubbing it with a piece of chalk and then erasing it.

5. Label each pail with the chalk marker.

Fill your pails with your gardening tools and supplies. Use these pails to store potting soil and birdseed, too. For added ease tie a small scoop to each handle.

Seed-Storage Box

For anyone with a green thumb—and even for those without one—this seed-storage box gives you a beautiful and practical way to store seeds from your garden or that you've purchased. Whether you save seeds from year to year or simply need a spot to write down and store information, seed packets, or plant tags, this can be your go-to spot to keep all that information safe and in one place. The dividers allow for added organization. The chalkboard lid helps you keep track of what seeds can be found in each divider as well as gives you extra space to record information you want to remember for next year's garden.

What You'll Need:

- Top: 1 piece of pine measuring 16" × 7¼" × ¾"
- Bottom: 1 piece of pine measuring 16" × 7¼" × ⅜"
- Front and back: 2 pieces of pine measuring 16" × 2¾" × ½"
- Sides: 2 pieces of pine measuring 6¼" × 2¾" × ½"
- Long main divider: 1 piece of pine measuring 15" × 2¾" × ⅜"
- Short dividers: 3 pieces of pine measuring 6¼" × 2¾" × ⅜"
- Kreg pocket hole jig system (including pocket hole drill guide, ⅜" stepped drill bit with depth collar, and #2 square driver)
- 8 pocket screws: 1" stainless steel pocket screws (optional as wood screws or nails could be used to secure the box together)
- Wood glue
- Clamps

- Brad nailer (or hammer and nails)
- ¾" brad nails
- Table saw (or circular saw or handsaw)
- Tape measure
- Pencil
- Sandpaper (150, 220 grit)
- Tack cloth
- 1" painter's tape
- WATCO Danish Oil
- Cheesecloth
- 2 narrow 1½" utility hinges
- 4 ⅜" screws (in the same finish as your hinges)
- Chalkboard paint
- 1" foam paintbrush
- Chalk

What You'll Do:

1. Using the pocket hole jig, drill 2 pocket holes on each end of the 2 short sides.

Note. **This box does not need to support a lot of weight, and therefore these pieces could also be joined using small screws or nails.**

2. Once the 8 pocket holes have been drilled on the short sides, join all 4 sides together, locating the 2 short side pieces between the front and back pieces. Run a bead of glue along the edges where the pieces meet, and clamp everything firmly in place. Fasten using the 8 pocket screws. Although pocket screws were used here, you can just as easily glue and then nail the pieces.

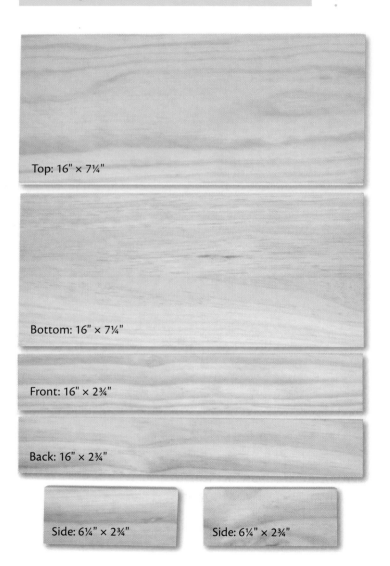

Top: 16" × 7¼"

Bottom: 16" × 7¼"

Front: 16" × 2¾"

Back: 16" × 2¾"

Side: 6¼" × 2¾"

Side: 6¼" × 2¾"

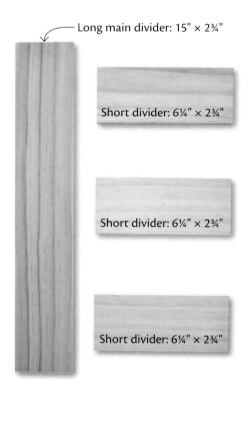

Long main divider: 15" × 2¾"

Short divider: 6¼" × 2¾"

Short divider: 6¼" × 2¾"

Short divider: 6¼" × 2¾"

3. Place the box frame you just created onto the bottom, flip the piece over, and fasten the bottom to the sides using wood glue and ¾" brad nails.

4. Next you will work on the dividers. I used ⅜" pine for the dividers because of its relative stability. Take the long middle divider (15" × 2¾") and measure 7½" from each end to mark the location of the center with your pencil.

5. Next, measure 3⅝" from each end and make 2 additional marks. These marks represent the location of the middle of the notches you will cut out. Center a ⅜"-thick piece of wood on each of these marks and with your pencil, make a mark on each side of the wood, giving you the width of the notch to cut out.

6. Measure 1⅜" from the bottom of the long board at the location of each notch. Connect the marks you made, forming a rectangle, which you will cut out using a table saw or small handsaw.

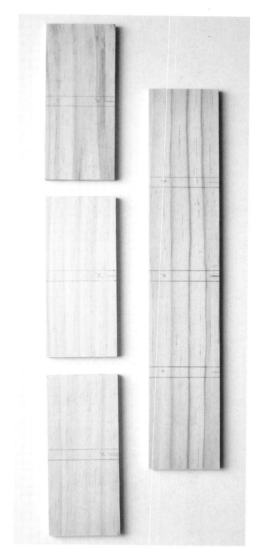

7. Locate the middle of the small dividers. Measure 3⅛" from each end to be sure you have found the middle. Again, center a ⅜"-thick piece of wood on each of these marks and with your pencil, make a mark on each side, giving you the width of the notch to cut out. Measure 1⅛" up the side of the small divider, locating the depth of the notch. Connect the marks you made, forming a rectangle, which you will cut out using a table saw or small handsaw.

8. Slide the dividers together and place them in the box to ensure a proper fit. If the fit is as desired, remove the dividers for finishing.

9. Next, take the piece designated as the top and round over the top edge on all 4 sides, using the 150-grit sandpaper working up to the 220 grit. This will soften the edge and give it a beautiful hand-finished look.

10. Remove any additional dust and debris with a tack cloth. Apply your desired finish. For this project, I used WATCO Danish Oil in Dark Walnut, but you can use any color that appeals to you. Apply using the cheesecloth and following manufacturer's directions. This type of finish is easy to apply and does not need any other protective finish unless it is desired. For example, you could use a clear satin polyurethane, following the manufacturer's directions.

11. Once everything is dry, reassemble the dividers, and place them back into the box. In order to allow them to be removed for cleaning, do not glue these into place.

12. Next, attach the hardware. Fasten narrow 1½" utility hinges located 2½" from each end on the back and inside top of the box to secure the cover to the base.

> **Note.** Make sure the screws going into the back of the box do not exceed ½", as they will come through the other side of the wood. It is likely that the screws that come with the hinges will be too long, so plan to purchase 4 ⅜" screws in the same finish as the hinge chosen for the back. You should be able to use the screws included with the hardware to attach the top, as it is thicker than the sides.

13. Decide what you would like to store your seeds in. I chose to paint some envelopes with a thin strip of chalkboard paint near the top of each one for a more uniform look. However, you could easily store seeds in the package they came in.

14. On the inside cover of the seed box, paint 2–3 coats of chalkboard paint. Be sure to read the manufacturer's instructions on the label for drying times in between each coat of paint.

15. Once the paint has dried, season the chalkboard portion of the seed box (and the chalkboard envelopes, if necessary) by rubbing it with a piece of chalk and then erasing it.

You are now ready to use your seed-storage box. Use the chalkboard underneath the cover to help you keep an inventory of heirloom seeds you have remaining or have planted in your garden. It will also be useful in documenting what seeds will need to be ordered for the next growing season.

CHAPTER SIX

The Organized Chalkboard

With all the chaos there is in our lives, it's nice to impose a little order—through chalkboards. Just think of all the opportunities they give you to label things. Bins and baskets! Jars and cans! Boxes and trays! This chapter offers some larger chalkboard projects, such as decorative storage boxes, a greeting card organizer, bookends, and an electronic docking station, as well as smaller projects, such as spice jars, clipboards, and linen closet labels.

Electronic Charging Station

Do you ever look at an outlet in your house, jammed with a rat's nest of tangled charging cords, and wonder how on earth to keep all your devices straight? This handy and attractive charging station solves your problem. The chalkboard front is useful for labeling which electronic device goes where; it can also remind older children of the time when they need to turn in their phones or tablets for the evening. The open section underneath the removable cover is large enough to accommodate a six-outlet power strip, keeping all of those plugs secure and out of sight. Say farewell to those tangled cords and cluttered counters!

What You'll Need:

- Platform blocking: 1 piece of pine measuring 11¼" × 1" × ⅜"
- Platform blocking: 2 pieces of pine measuring 5¼" × 1" × ⅜"
- Front riser: 1 piece of pine measuring 12" × 1½" × ⅜"
- Top: 1 piece of pine measuring 12½" × 2½" × ½"
- Back: 1 piece of pine measuring 12" × 4" × ⅜"
- Back riser: 1 piece of pine measuring 11¼" × 2¾" × ⅜"
- Platform: 1 piece of plywood measuring 11¼" × 5¾" × ¼"
- Platform blocking: 1 piece of pine measuring 6" × 1" × ⅜"

- Wood glue
- Clamps
- Side curved pieces: 2 pieces of pine that begin measuring 7½" × 4" × ⅜" (The back starts at 4" and extends out 2 ¹⁄₁₆" at the 4" height to accommodate the width of the power strip and curves down to match the front at 1½" (see photo).
- Small wood blocks: 2 pieces of pine measuring 1½" × 1¼" × ⅜"
- Tape measure
- Pencil
- Scroll saw (or ¼" drill bit and metal files)

- Jigsaw
- Sandpaper (150, 220 grit)
- Brad nailer (or hammer and nails)
- ¾" brad nails
- Coping saw
- Wood filler
- Tack cloth
- White semigloss paint
- Chalkboard paint
- Painter's tape (1")
- 2 1" foam paintbrushes
- Chalk

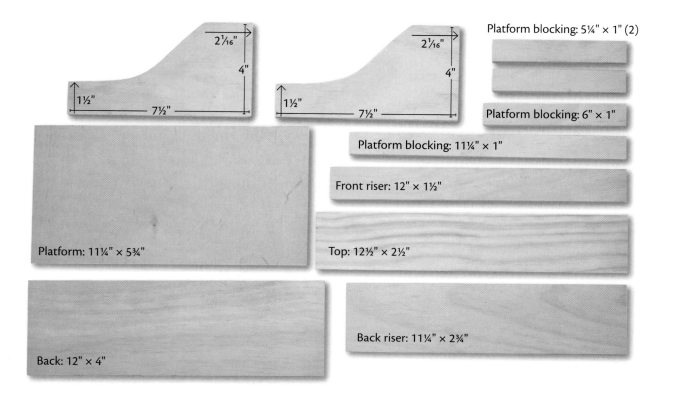

2¹/₁₆"

4"

1½"

7½"

2¹/₁₆"

4"

1½"

7½"

Platform blocking: 5¼" × 1" (2)

Platform blocking: 6" × 1"

Platform blocking: 11¼" × 1"

Front riser: 12" × 1½"

Platform: 11¼" × 5¾"

Top: 12½" × 2½"

Back: 12" × 4"

Back riser: 11¼" × 2¾"

What You'll Do:

1. In the platform piece of plywood, cut rectangular openings measuring ¹/₁₆" × ⁵/₁₆" and located 1" from the back edge of the plywood. Space these openings evenly, at ¾" apart, starting 1½" from the left/right end. A total of 5 were created here, but the number can vary. This is where the power cord for each device will come through.

2. On the underside of the platform, attach the ⅜" pine platform blocking using wood glue. Attach the 11¼" × 1" piece on the front underside, the 5¼" × 1" pieces on the left and right undersides, and the 6" × 1" piece centered underneath the back edge. Clamp together and let dry until the glue is set. Be sure to read the label for drying times.

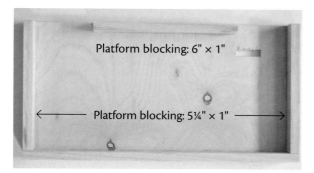

Platform blocking: 6" × 1"

Platform blocking: 5¼" × 1"

3. Next, prepare the sides using the template from the Appendix. Make a copy of the template and cut it out. Tape it to a piece of ⅜" pine that measures 7½" × 4". Trace the outline of the template onto the board. Once you are satisfied with the tracing, tape the board with the tracing on it to the other 7½" × 4" side board. Make sure the boards are securely held together. Clamp both boards, now evenly stacked, to your work surface. Using a jigsaw, cut on the outside of the pencil line as close to it as possible. While the boards are still together, sand both pieces using 120- and 150-grit sandpaper until the desired curve and smoothness is achieved. Finish with 220-grit sandpaper, if necessary.

4. Dry fit the back (12" × 4"), front riser (12" × 1½"), and curved sides around the platform. If the fit is as desired, glue these pieces and hold them in place with clamps. For extra reinforcement, nail them together using ¾" brad nails. Allow the glue to dry according to the manufacturer's directions.

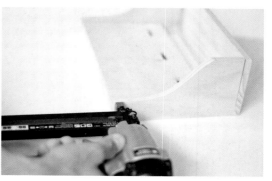

5. Once all of the sides are attached to the platform, position the back riser (11¼" × 2¾") on the back of the platform. If the fit is as desired, remove it, run a bead of wood glue down the ends, and set it into its final position, making sure it is perpendicular to the platform. Secure the back riser using ¾" brad nails from the sides. Allow the glue to dry according to the manufacturer's directions.

6. Attach two small wood blocks (each 1½" × 1¼") to the underside of the top (12½" × 2½") using wood glue and ¾" brad nails. Locate each block ⅜" from the front and back edges of the top and ¹¹⁄₁₆" from each end. These blocks function to keep the top in place, while allowing it to be lifted off at any time to access the cords.

7. Using a small handsaw, such as a coping saw, create a ½" × ½" notch on the back at the bottom for the power cord on either the left or right side.

8. Fill in any nail holes and imperfections with wood filler. Sand the entire piece using 150-grit sandpaper, rounding over the edges to soften them if desired. To prepare the charging station for paint, finish sanding with the 220-grit sandpaper and then clean up any dust and debris with the tack cloth.

9. Paint the entire charging station with 2–3 coats of white semigloss paint. Be sure to read the manufacturer's instructions on the label for drying times between each coat of paint. Allow the final coat of paint to dry overnight.

10. Using the painter's tape, tape off the front riser. Take care to firmly press down the tape so that paint will not leak underneath.

11. Apply 2–3 coats of chalkboard paint to the front riser. Be sure to read the manufacturer's instructions on the label for drying times in between each coat of paint.

12. After the paint has dried, season the chalkboard portion of the charging station by rubbing it with a piece of chalk and then erasing it.

You are now ready to place the power strip and your cords inside the charging station and to write on the chalkboard portion, keeping both your life and your electronics more organized.

GREETING CARD ORGANIZER

In this age of e-mail and Twitter, getting an actual handwritten sentiment from someone is less and less common. This greeting card organizer can serve to inspire you to shop for meaningful cards, keep them organized in an attractive way, and send them to those you love.

What You'll Need:

- ○ Front and back: 2 pieces of pine measuring 20" × 4¼" × ⅜"
- ○ Sides: 2 pieces of pine measuring 5" × 4" × ⅜"
- ○ Bottom: 1 piece of plywood measuring 20" × 6¾" × ¼"
- ○ Dividers: 2 pieces of pine measuring 5" × 4" × ⅜"
- ○ Small trim molding: Measuring approximately 60" to accommodate the miter cuts and the waste from each cut
- ○ Table saw
- ○ Compound miter saw (optional)
- ○ Brad nailer (or hammer and nails)
- ○ ¾" brad nails (or ¾" pin nails)
- ○ Clamps
- ○ Wood glue
- ○ Tape measure
- ○ Pencil
- ○ Wood filler
- ○ Sandpaper (120, 150 grit)
- ○ Tack cloth
- ○ White semigloss paint
- ○ 1" painter's tape
- ○ Chalkboard paint
- ○ 2 1" foam paintbrushes
- ○ Chalk

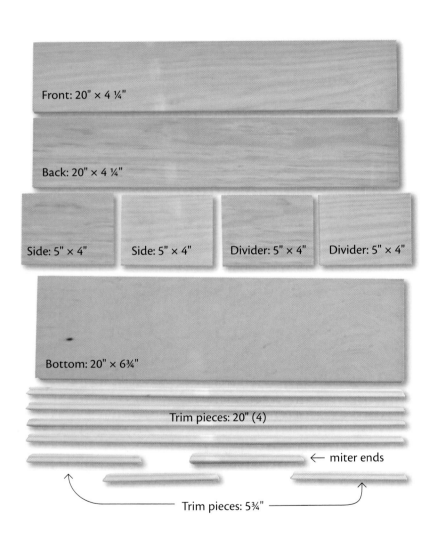

Front: 20" × 4 ¼"

Back: 20" × 4 ¼"

Side: 5" × 4" Side: 5" × 4" Divider: 5" × 4" Divider: 5" × 4"

Bottom: 20" × 6¾"

Trim pieces: 20" (4)

← miter ends

Trim pieces: 5¾"

What You'll Do:

1. First, construct a box. Dry fit the two sides (5" × 4") between the front and back (20" × 4¼"). Glue the edges where they meet, clamp the sides firmly together, and nail together using ¾" brad nails.

2. Line up and attach the bottom using wood glue and ¾" brad nails.

3. Measure 6¹¹⁄₁₆" from each end on the top of the front board (20" × 4¼") and make a mark with your pencil. These marks will line up with the center of each divider and will help you to align the dividers properly. Repeat this process for the back board.

4. Measure along the top width of each of the small dividers and locate the center. Make a mark with the pencil at this center location on both ends so you can easily match up these marks with those you made on the long sides of the box when you position the dividers within the box.

5. Install the dividers using the location marks you made on these pieces. Glue and nail the dividers in place using ¾" brad nails or pin nails.

6. Finish the top and bottom of the box off with the small trim molding mitered at the corners and securing it using wood glue and ¾" brad nails.

7. Fill in any nail holes or gaps with wood filler. Be sure to read the label to determine how long it will take for the wood filler to dry.

8. Remove any rough edges and sides by sanding the entire piece beginning with the 150-grit and ending with the 220-grit sandpaper. Use the tack cloth to remove any dust or debris.

9. Paint the entire greeting card organizer using 2–3 coats of the white semigloss paint. Be sure to read the manufacturer's instructions on the label to learn how long to wait for drying times between each coat of paint. Allow the final coat of paint to dry overnight.

10. Using the painter's tape, tape off three 3" × 2" rectangles centered in front of each compartment.

11. Inside of each rectangle, apply 2–3 coats of the chalkboard paint. Be sure to read the manufacturer's instructions on the label for drying times between each coat of paint.

12. When the chalkboard paint has dried, season each rectangle by rubbing it with a piece of chalk and then erasing it.

Decide how you would like to organize your greeting cards. Label each section and place the cards inside.

Do not limit this greeting card organizer to greeting cards. Use it to organize incoming and outgoing mail. Fill each compartment with smaller canisters and store stamps, paper clips, or even crafting supplies.

DESKTOP STORAGE CONTAINERS

You don't need anything leather-covered or expensive to organize that pile of pens, pencils, paper clips, and goodness knows what else that's cluttering up your desk. Reuse some tin cans from your kitchen and turn them into desktop storage containers. By adding a chalkboard element to them, you'll be able to label, organize, decorate, and change them to your heart's content, all while giving you a stylish look.

What You'll Need:

- ○ 3 tin cans
- ○ Gold or silver spray paint
- ○ 1" painter's tape
- ○ Chalkboard paint
- ○ 1" foam paintbrush
- ○ Chalk

What You'll Do:

1. Wash and dry the tin cans thoroughly.

2. In a well-ventilated area, spray both the inside and outside of the tin cans with 2–3 thin coats of the spray paint. Be sure to read the manufacturer's instructions on the label for drying times in between each coat of paint.

3. After the spray paint has dried, tape off the top ridged portion of the tin cans. The flat portion at the very top of the can is where you will apply the chalkboard paint.

4. Paint the cans with 2–3 coats of chalkboard paint, using the foam paintbrush. Be sure to read the manufacturer's instructions on the label for drying times in between each coat of paint.

5. Season the chalkboard portion of the cans by rubbing with a piece of chalk and then erasing it.

You are now ready to fill your storage container and label the contents. Feel free to substitute any type of canister or container if tin cans are not your style.

PAPERWEIGHT

Hold down your most important papers and use the chalkboard portion to keep track of due dates, meetings, or other friendly reminders with this stylish chalkboard paperweight. This project truly gives meaning to the phrase "style meets function." Choose any wood or resin figurine that appeals to you. Make sure there is a sufficient amount of space to do some writing on the figurine you choose.

What You'll Need:

- ○ Wood, resin, or plastic figurine
- ○ Chalkboard spray paint
- ○ 1" painter's tape
- ○ Paint pen (silver, or another fun accent color)
- ○ Chalk

What You'll Do:

1. Give 2–3 thin coats of spray paint to your figurine in a well-ventilated area. Be sure to read the manufacturer's instructions on the label for drying times in between each coat of paint.

2. Now is the time to get a little creative with your paperweight. Using the paint pen, draw some fun accents onto your paperweight to give it a little visual interest. I chose to tape off a small portion above the pig's feet. I then used a silver paint pen to color each of the feet. Be creative but make sure to leave some room for chalk.

3. After you have finished embellishing your paperweight, season the entire surface with a piece of chalk by rubbing it and then erasing it.

You are now ready to write on and use your chalkboard paperweight.

Wouldn't these be fun as gift tags tied to the tops of presents?

CLIPBOARDS

Do you crave organization? Do you have a difficult time keeping track of your spouse's and children's busy schedules? If so, add some chalkboard clipboards into your home décor. If you have a little wall space in your home office, kitchen, or mudroom, this idea will give you the organization you need. The back portion of the clipboard can be used to keep track of meetings, practices, and appointments. The clip portion of the clipboard can hold notes, permission slips, bills, or receipts. When placed in a small grouping, it is a stylish way to keep order in your busy life.

What You'll Need:

- ○ 4 clipboards
- ○ 1" painter's tape
- ○ Chalkboard spray paint
- ○ 4 screw hooks
- ○ Chalk

What You'll Do:

1. Tape off the metal clip portion of the clipboard as well as any other portions of the clipboard you wish to remain free of paint.

2. Using the chalkboard spray paint, spray 2–3 thin coats to the clipboard. Let each coat of paint dry before applying the next. Be sure to read the manufacturer's instructions on the label for drying times in between each coat of paint.

3. When the paint has dried, hang each clipboard with a screw hook in a grouping. The screw hook will allow the clipboard to be removed easily.

4. To season the clipboard, rub a small piece of chalk over the entire chalkboard surface and then erase the chalk.

You are now ready to use your chalkboard clipboard.

Desire even more organization? Designate one clipboard for each member of your family. With this simple organizational trick, everyone can take a quick glance at their clipboard before heading out the door for the day and be off to a good start.

Linen-Closet Labels

Make finding and putting away the sheets, towels, and toiletries in your linen closet that much easier with some attractive baskets labeled with chalkboard labels. Since baskets hold and hide almost anything that you can think of, they are the perfect containers for a linen closet. It's a great feeling to open the door of a well-organized closet that looks beautiful!

What You'll Need:

- ○ Wood craft rectangles (size and number to be determined by you)
- ○ Baskets (number to be determined by you)
- ○ Drill
- ○ Drill bit (⅛")
- ○ Chalkboard spray paint
- ○ Twine or ribbon
- ○ Chalk

What You'll Do:

1. Drill two small holes on each side of the wood craft rectangles big enough for the ribbon to go through.

2. Spray 2–3 thin coats of chalkboard spray paint onto the sides and edges of each wood craft rectangle. Be sure to read the manufacturer's instructions on the label for drying times in between each coat of paint.

3. Once the paint has dried, thread the twine through the holes on the chalkboard labels and attach them to the baskets.

4. Season the chalkboard labels by rubbing with a piece of chalk and then erasing it.

You are now ready to write on your labels and fill your baskets with whatever might need organizing in your linen closet.

You can organize any closet in your home with a few baskets and some chalkboard labels. Organize the kids' closets that way, and let them make their own labels.

BOOKENDS

Who was it who said you can never have too many books? These chalkboard bookends are a great place to record what types of books or magazines are on your bookshelves. The flat portion on each bookend lets you to write down anything you want, from categories to topics. The polyurethane finish chosen for this project echoes the simple, modern style. However, feel free to substitute your favorite color of finish to make this project your own.

What You'll Need:

- ○ Vertical side: 2 pieces of pine measuring 7¼" × 3½" × ¾"
- ○ Bottom: 2 pieces of pine measuring 6¼" × 3½" × ¾"
- ○ Back: 2 pieces of pine measuring 7¼" × 7" × ¾"
- ○ Tape measure
- ○ Pencil
- ○ Drill
- ○ Kreg pocket screw jig system (including pocket hole drill guide, ⅜" stepped drill bit with depth collar, and #2 square driver)
- ○ 8 pocket screws
- ○ 4 1¼" wood screws
- ○ Clamps
- ○ Wood glue
- ○ Sandpaper (150, 220 grit)
- ○ Tack cloth
- ○ 1" painter's tape
- ○ Clear gloss fast-drying polyurethane
- ○ Chalkboard paint
- ○ 2 1" foam paintbrushes
- ○ Chalk

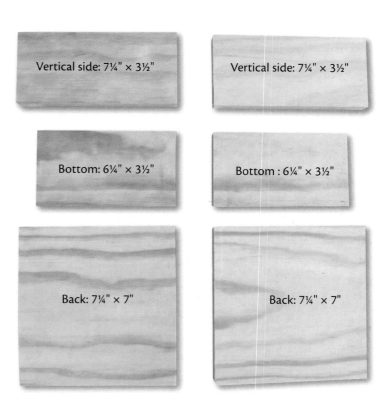

Vertical side: 7¼" × 3½"

Vertical side: 7¼" × 3½"

Bottom: 6¼" × 3½"

Bottom : 6¼" × 3½"

Back: 7¼" × 7"

Back: 7¼" × 7"

What You'll Do:

1. Drill 4 pocket holes on the bottom of the 6¼" × 3½" piece on 2 sides perpendicular to each other (2 on each side located near the ends). This will become the bottom of the bookend.

2. Match the edge of the 7¼" × 3½" piece with the bottom, creating an "L" shape. Lay the "L" shaped piece on the 7¼" × 7" piece to make sure everything fits.

3. Glue and clamp the 3 pieces together and secure using pocket screws. Attach the back to the vertical piece of the bookend from behind using screws.

4. Once both bookends are assembled, sand the faces and edges to remove any rough spots, starting with the 150-grit sandpaper and finishing with 220 grit.

5. Use the tack cloth to remove any dust or debris.

6. Next, apply painter's tape to the back panel of each bookend to prevent any polyurethane from getting onto them.

7. With a foam paintbrush, apply the polyurethane to the small pieces that form each "L". For best results, follow the manufacturer's instructions, which will help you determine how many coats to use as well as how long it will take for the polyurethane to dry.

8. Once the polyurethane has dried, apply painter's tape to those areas to prevent any chalkboard paint from leaking onto it.

9. Paint 2–3 coats of chalkboard paint to the back panel. Be sure to read the manufacturer's instructions on the label for drying times in between each coat of paint.

10. Once the paint has dried, season both back panels with a piece of chalk and then erase it.

You are now ready to write on your chalkboard bookends.

If you do not care for the look of the stained wood, feel free to paint that portion of the bookend in any color you choose!

SPICE JARS

Spice up your life! Make your spice cupboard or drawer more organized and pleasing to the eye with these chalkboard spice jars. Since these labels are not made from paper, you don't have to worry about any spills or splatters. Simply wipe away the mess and the chalk, rewrite the name of the herb, and tuck the jars safely away.

What You'll Need:

- ○ Glass spice jars (number to be determined by you)
- ○ 1" painter's tape
- ○ Multisurface chalkboard paint (gray)
- ○ 1" foam paintbrush
- ○ Chalk
- ○ Chalk marker

What You'll Do:

1. Wash and dry each spice jar thoroughly.

2. Next, tape off a small section around the entire spice jar using the painter's tape. This is desirable so that you can see the label as well as the herbs inside.

3. Paint 2–3 thin coats of the chalkboard paint onto each spice jar. Be sure to read the manufacturer's instructions on the label for drying times in between each coat of paint.

4. After the paint has dried, season the surface of each spice jar by rubbing it with a piece of chalk and then erasing it.

5. Fill each jar with an herb and then write the name of the herb on the label.

To keep your chalkboard labels nice for years to come, I recommend hand washing and drying your jars. These spice jars, along with some favorite family recipes, make a sweet and unique house-warming or bridal shower gift!

Decorative Storage Boxes

When it comes to storage options in your home, think beyond boring plastic storage bins and baskets. When sturdy wooden boxes are combined with some chalkboard labels, storage has never looked better! These decorative storage bins will be ones that you can proudly display amongst your other décor.

What You'll Need:

- ○ Wooden craft storage boxes (number to be determined by you)
- ○ Sandpaper (150, 220 grit)
- ○ Tack cloth
- ○ Clear-gloss fast-drying polyurethane
- ○ Chalkboard paint
- ○ 2 1" foam paintbrushes
- ○ Label stencil
- ○ Chalk
- ○ Chalk marker

What You'll Do:

1. Sand each box with the sandpaper to remove any rough areas on the sides and edges. Once you have finished sanding, remove any dust and debris by wiping the box with the tack cloth.

2. Choose one side of the box to apply chalkboard paint to and use painter's tape to protect that side.

3. Apply the polyurethane with a foam paintbrush to the three remaining sides, the inside, and the bottom of each box. For best results, follow the manufacturer's instructions, which will help you

determine how many coats to use as well as how long it will take for the polyurethane to dry, especially since you will be applying painter's tape to these areas in the next step.

4. After the polyurethane has dried, tape off the sides and edges so that you do not get any chalkboard paint on them.

5. Paint 2–3 thin coats of chalkboard paint to the remaining side of the box. Be sure to read the manufacturer's instructions on the label for drying times in between each coat of paint.

6. Season the chalkboard portion of the decorative storage box by rubbing with a piece of chalk and then erasing it.

7. Once the chalkboard paint has dried, place the label stencil onto the chalkboard portion and then tape it into place. Use the chalk marker to fill in the stencil. The chalk marker will make the label more permanent.

Display these storage boxes on your bookshelf or console table shelf. They would also be darling stacked on top of one another on the floor!

CHAPTER SEVEN

Holiday Fun

This chapter will inspire you to incorporate chalkboard paint into any season and holiday. Projects such as an acorn garland, a pumpkin, and a thankful tree will give you bountiful opportunities to use chalkboards all fall long. The Christmas holiday is even cheerier when you make a chalkboard Advent calendar. Finally, you can incorporate chalkboard crafts into Valentine's Day, Easter, and the Fourth of July. Happy Holidays to you!

PUMPKIN

I don't think anything says Halloween quite like a jack-o'-lantern. When you paint a pumpkin with chalkboard paint, you have a surface that can be decorated over and over again! Whether these chalkboard pumpkins are adorned with spooky or funny faces, they are a sure way to get you in a festive mood.

What You'll Need:

- Pumpkin (faux)
- 1" painter's tape (optional)
- Chalkboard paint
- 1" foam paintbrush
- Chalk

What You'll Do:

1. If you want people to see some of the beautiful color on the pumpkin, use the painter's tape to keep any paint off those areas.

2. Apply 2–3 thin coats of chalkboard paint to the pumpkin. Be sure to read the manufacturer's instructions on the label for drying times in between each coat of paint.

3. Once the paint has dried, season the surface by rubbing it with a piece of chalk and then erasing it.

4. You are now ready to decorate your chalkboard pumpkin!

If you are hosting a Halloween party, especially for little ones, allowing all of your guests to decorate a pumpkin and then take it home would be an especially fun and appropriate activity.

ACORN GARLAND

I think the most wonderful thing about fall is the abundance of natural elements you can bring inside to decorate your home, whether they are pumpkins, leaves, gourds, or nuts. This rustic acorn garland is an easy way to bring the outdoors in. It will allow you to decorate your table or mantel during the season without fussing too much. The chalkboard element allows you to customize the garland throughout the season, from the start of fall all the way to Thanksgiving.

What You'll Need:

- Twine
- Measuring tape
- Acorns (faux or real)
- Scissors
- Chalkboard paint
- 1" foam paintbrush
- Chalk
- Hot glue gun
- Glue sticks

What You'll Do:

1. Measure how long your garland should be. Allow an extra foot or two so you can drape the garland as well as tie some knots to secure the acorns.

2. Cut the twine to your desired length and set aside.

3. Next, decide what you would like your garland to say. You will need to allow one acorn for each letter of your message. Remember, if you chose to write more than one word on your garland, such as "Harvest Time" or "Happy Thanksgiving," you will need to allow for one acorn to serve as a spacer so that your message will be able to be read.

4. Paint the bottom of each acorn with 2–3 coats of chalkboard paint. This garland is supposed to look a little rustic, so don't worry too much about perfection or straight lines on the acorns. Be sure to read the manufacturer's instructions on the label for drying times in between each coat of paint.

5. Once the acorns have dried, season each one by rubbing it with a piece of chalk and then erasing it.

6. If there are large stems on top of each acorn, you should be able to tie a knot with the twine around the top. If not, you will need to glue the twine to the top of each acorn.

7. Once you have all of your chalkboard acorns secured to the twine, you are ready to write on them. Write a letter on each acorn to spell out a festive message like "harvest" or "Thanksgiving."

Display the acorn garland in an area of your home where you can enjoy it all fall long.

Feel free to substitute any outdoor fall item that you choose, such as preserved leaves or gourds.

THANKFUL TREE

Count your blessings with your family and friends during Thanksgiving with this chalkboard thankful tree. This project makes a stunningly beautiful centerpiece at your table and will remind your guests of the true meaning of the holiday. Place the chalkboard leaves in a pretty bowl next to the tree with some pieces of chalk. Let your guests write down what they are thankful for and hang them on the tree. It will be a memory to be thankful for!

What You'll Need:

- ○ Parchment paper
- ○ Oven-bake clay
- ○ Crafting rolling pin
- ○ Small leaf cookie cutter (or any shape that you desire and is appropriate for Thanksgiving)
- ○ Metal cookie sheet
- ○ Wooden skewer
- ○ Silver accent paint
- ○ Chalkboard paint
- ○ 1 1" foam paintbrushes
- ○ Chalk
- ○ String or ribbon
- ○ Sticks or branches
- ○ Silver spray paint (optional)
- ○ Large vase

What You'll Do:

1. To begin, protect your work surface with the parchment paper and make sure that your hands are clean.

2. Take a portion of clay and work it in your hands to soften it. Roll it into a ball and then place it on your work surface. Using the rolling pin, roll the clay to a ¼" thickness.

3. Cut out some leaf shapes with the leaf cookie cutter. Carefully place the leaf shapes on a parchment paper–covered cookie sheet.

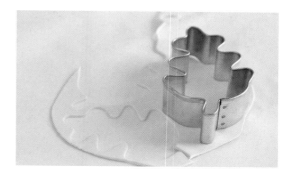

4. Using the wooden skewer, make a hole big enough for your string or ribbon at the top of each clay tag. Bake the clay leaves according to the clay manufacturer's instructions and let them cool completely before removing them from the baking sheet.

5. After the leaves have cooled and hardened, place them back onto your work surface. Using a 1" foam paintbrush, paint one side of each leaf with the silver accent paint. Give each leaf a couple of coats of paint and sufficient time to dry between each coat. Be sure to read the manufacturer's instructions on the label for drying times in between each coat of paint.

6. When the silver paint has dried, paint the other side of each leaf with 2–3 coats of chalkboard paint. Be sure to read the label for drying times in between each coat of paint.

7. Take a piece of chalk and rub the chalkboard surface to season it. Erase the chalk completely.

8. Next, cut the string or ribbon to your desired length and thread it through the hole. You are now ready to write your blessings on your chalkboard leaves.

9. Once you are done with the chalkboard leaves, you can assemble the "tree" on which you will hang them. I chose to spray paint my sticks and branches a silver color, but leaving them in their natural state would also be lovely. Place the sticks and branches in the vase and then hang the chalkboard leaves on the branches after you and your guests have written on them.

Create a new family tradition! At the end of the Thanksgiving holiday, pack the leaves away with the rest of your decorations to be used again next year.

ADVENT CALENDAR

Everyone knows that to a child, **Christmas Day** seems to take forever to come! Counting down to that very special day will be even more memorable when you give them something to look forward to each day—like an **Advent** calendar. By opening a little box each day filled with some small treat, ornament, or sentiment, they will have something to look forward to until December 25.

What You'll Need:

- ○ 25 small cardboard craft boxes 2½" × 2½" × 1½"
- ○ Chalkboard paint
- ○ 1" foam paintbrush
- ○ Small and medium foam circle stencil brushes
- ○ 50 silver thumbtacks
- ○ Large corkboard, measuring roughly 3' × 2'
- ○ Items to decorate the corkboard, such as ribbon, Washi tape, and wreaths
- ○ Chalk
- ○ Chalk marker

What You'll Do:

1. Separate the covers of each box from the bottoms.

2. Paint the covers of each box with 1–2 thin coats of chalkboard paint with the foam paintbrush. Be sure to read the manufacturer's instructions on the label for drying times in between each coat of paint.

3. Using the small- and medium-size stencil brushes, stencil polka dots onto the sides of each box.

4. While the polka dots are drying, decorate the corkboard in order to make it look more festive. I chose to use Washi tape on the wood frame and hang a boxwood wreath at the top with some ribbon. Be creative and use things that are meaningful to you.

5. When the painted polka dots have dried, evenly space each box onto the corkboard. Use the thumbtacks to pin each box into place.

6. Season each chalkboard cover by rubbing it with a piece of chalk and then erasing it.

7. Label each cover with the numbers 1–25, using the chalk marker.

8. Fill each box and then place the covers back onto each box. You are now ready to celebrate all through December!

If you are unsure about using a corkboard for this project, you can substitute a painted piece of plywood and secure the boxes using hot glue.

Simple Valentine

A heart is the quintessential shape of Valentine's Day. Give the ones you love a Valentine straight from your heart, complete with a space for you to write down just how much they mean to you. Place this chalkboard heart in a pretty little glassine or vellum envelope with a few sweets and a brand-new piece of chalk. With this simple Valentine, you will steal their hearts!

What You'll Need:

- ○ Wooden craft heart (or cut out your own from a piece of ¼" or ⅜" wood)
- ○ Chalkboard spray paint
- ○ Red, white, and pink chalk
- ○ Washi tape
- ○ Vellum or glassine envelope
- ○ Candy

What You'll Do:

1. In a well-ventilated space, spray the sides and edge of the wooden heart with 2–3 coats of chalkboard spray paint. Be sure to read the manufacturer's instructions on the label for drying times in between each coat of paint.

2. Once the paint has dried, season the heart with a piece of chalk by rubbing it and then erasing it.

3. Take a new piece of chalk and fasten it to the heart with a piece of Washi tape.

4. Using the colored chalk, write a message and decorate the heart.

5. Tuck the chalkboard heart Valentine into the vellum or glassine envelope, along with some sweets, and then seal the envelope closed with another piece of Washi tape.

You are now ready to give your heart to your Valentine!

Clay Spring Gift Tags

These spring gift tags are a cute way of decorating an Easter basket or adding a special touch to a gift for a sweet, spring newborn baby. Since light and bright colors are reminiscent of spring, using pastel chalkboard paint is a cheery and appropriate choice!

What You'll Need:

- ○ Parchment paper
- ○ Oven-bake clay
- ○ Crafting rolling pin
- ○ Small spring cookie cutters, (e.g., rabbit, chick, or egg shapes)
- ○ Metal cookie sheet
- ○ Wooden skewer
- ○ Pastel chalkboard paint
- ○ 1" foam paintbrush
- ○ Chalk
- ○ String or ribbon

What You'll Do:

1. Protect your work surface with the parchment paper and make sure that your hands are clean.

2. Take a portion of clay and work it in your hands to soften it. Roll it into a ball and then place it on your work surface. Using the rolling pin, roll the clay out to ¼" thickness.

3. With your cookie cutters, cut out your desired shapes. Carefully lift the clay shapes up and place them on a parchment paper–covered cookie sheet.

4. Using the wooden skewer, make a hole big enough for your string or ribbon at the top of each clay tag.

5. Bake your clay tags according to the manufacturer's instructions and let them cool completely before removing them from the baking sheet.

6. After the tags have cooled and hardened, place them back onto your work surface. Using the foam paintbrush, paint the entire surface of the tags with 1–2 coats of the pastel chalkboard paint. Be sure to read the manufacturer's instructions on the label for drying times in between each coat of paint.

7. After the paint has dried, take a piece of chalk and rub the entire surface of each gift tag. Erase the chalk completely.

8. Cut the string or ribbon to your desired length and thread it through the hole. You are now ready to write on your gift tags and attach them to an Easter basket or gift!

These simple gift tags could be used for any season or holiday. Simply switch the cookie cutters and chalkboard paint colors and you are ready for gift giving, whatever the season or reason!

Patriotic Lanterns

Nothing says summer or the Fourth of July quite like a barbecue that goes into the evening. Before those fireworks show up in the nighttime sky, let these patriotic lanterns shed a little light on your party. Though quick and inexpensive, they can make quite the statement.

What You'll Need:

- ○ 3 Mason jars
- ○ 1" painter's tape
- ○ Chalkboard paint
- ○ 1" foam paintbrush
- ○ 22-gauge silver wire
- ○ Wire cutters
- ○ Needle-nose pliers
- ○ Chalk
- ○ Red, white, and blue chalk markers
- ○ 3 battery-operated LED tea lights

What You'll Do:

1. Tape off about 1½" (enough to hide the flameless tea-light candles) at the bottom of each Mason jar, using the painter's tape.

2. Paint 2–3 thin coats of chalkboard paint onto each of the Mason jars.

3. While the final coat of paint dries, cut a piece of wire long enough to wrap around the mouth of the jar, plus a little extra to twist the ends together. Fasten the 2 ends of the wire together by twisting them with the needle-nose pliers. The ends of the wire can be sharp, so be careful! Repeat these steps for the remaining two jars.

4. Next, cut 1 more piece of wire to roughly 10" or so. This will be used to make the handle of the lantern. Make a "rainbow" shape with each piece of wire and attach each end to the other piece of wire securely with the needle-nose pliers. Repeat these steps for the remaining two jars.

5. Season the chalkboard portion of each lantern by rubbing it with a piece of chalk and then erasing it.

6. Using the red, white, and blue chalk markers, decorate each lantern. Why not draw a few stars and stripes on them? Or draw some fireworks, flags, or a patriotic phrase? Have fun and use your imagination.

7. Place the battery-powered LED tea-light candles inside each jar and enjoy your patriotic lanterns.

Light up the sky by hanging these from your pergola, patio umbrella, or a tree. Even placing them along a path or on a table would lend a patriotic and festive feel to your barbecue.

Templates

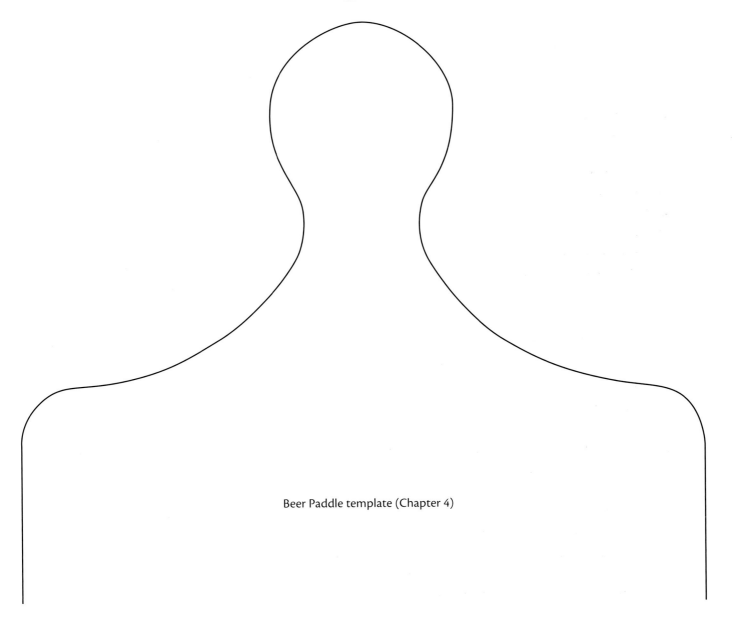

Beer Paddle template (Chapter 4)

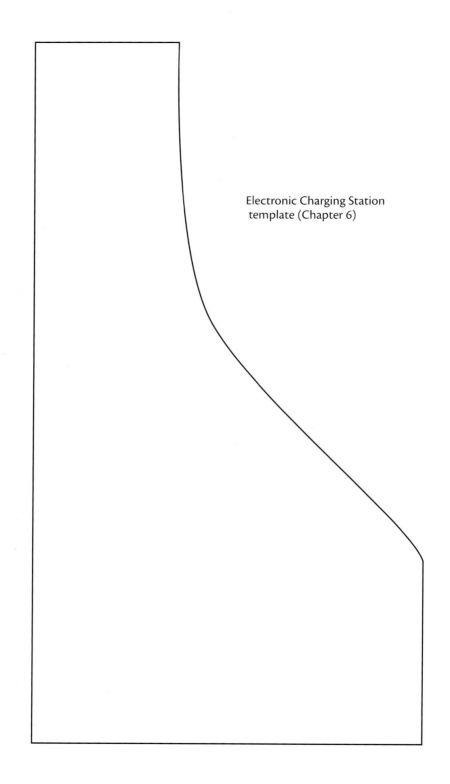

Electronic Charging Station
template (Chapter 6)

Index

Note: Page numbers in *italics* indicate projects.

About the Author

LIZETTE SCHAPEKAHM is the wife to Jason and mom to Henry, Oliver, and a little girl expected to arrive sometime in late 2013. A former teacher turned stay-at-home mom, photographer, crafter, blogger, home decorator, and DIY-er, she and her family live in Milwaukee, Wisconsin, in their little fixer-upper Cape Cod home. When she isn't busy taking care of her young family, she enjoys a good project, whether it be crafting, building, or sewing.

To learn more about Lizette and her projects, you can follow along on her blog, *Just So Lovely* (*www.justourlovelylife.blogspot.com/p/about-me.html*). She would be so glad if you did!